THE GILDED AGE & THE PROGRESSIVE ERA

History SparkNotes

Copyright © 2005 by Spark Educational Publishing

All rights reserved. No part of this book may be used or reproduced in any manner whatsoever without the written permission of the Publisher.

SPARKNOTES is a registered trademark of SparkNotes LLC

Spark Educational Publishing
A Division of Barnes & Noble Publishing
120 Fifth Avenue
New York, NY 10011
www.sparknotes.com

ISBN 1-4114-0424-6

Please submit all comments and questions or report errors to *www.sparknotes.com/errors*.

Printed and bound in the United States

CONTENTS

OVERVIEW

The Gilded Age and the first years of the twentieth century were a time of great social change and economic growth in the United States. Roughly spanning the years between Reconstruction and the dawn of the new century, the Gilded Age saw rapid industrialization, urbanization, the construction of great transcontinental railroads, innovations in science and technology, and the rise of big business. Afterward, the first years of the new century that followed were dominated by progressivism, a forward-looking political movement that attempted to redress some of the ills that had arisen during the Gilded Age. Progressives passed legislation to rein in big business, combat corruption, free the government from special interests, and protect the rights of consumers, workers, immigrants, and the poor.

Some historians have dubbed the presidents of the Gilded Age the "forgotten presidents," and indeed many Americans today have trouble remembering their names, what they did for the country, or even in which era they served. These six men—Ulysses S. Grant, Rutherford B. Hayes, James Garfield, Chester Arthur, Grover Cleveland, and Benjamin Harrison—had relatively unremarkable terms in office and faced few if any major national crises during their presidencies. Some historians have suggested that these Gilded Age presidents were unexciting for a reason—because Americans wanted to avoid bold politicians who might ruin the delicate peace established after the Civil War.

This is not to say politics were unimportant in the Gilded Age. On the contrary, Americans paid more attention to politics and national elections during the post–Civil War period than at any other time in history, because each election had the potential to disrupt the fragile balance—and peace—between North and South, Republican and Democrat. Voters turned out in record numbers for each presidential election in the late nineteenth century, with voter turnout sometimes reaching 80 percent or greater. The intensity of the elections also helps explain why Congress passed so little significant legislation after the Reconstruction era: control of the House of Representatives constantly changed hands between the Democrats and the Republicans with each election, making a consensus on any major issue nearly impossible.

The increase in voter turnout was also partly the result of machine party politics, which blossomed in large U.S. cities during the Gilded

Age. Powerful political "bosses" in each party coerced urban residents into voting for favored candidates, who would then give kickbacks and bribes back to the bosses in appreciation for getting them elected. Bosses would also spend money to improve constituents' neighborhoods to ensure a steady flow of votes for their machines. In this sense, party bosses and machine politics actually helped some of the poorest people in the cities. Many politicians elected during the Gilded Age were the product of machine party politics.

Driven by the North, which emerged from the Civil War an industrial powerhouse, the United States experienced a flurry of unprecedented growth and industrialization during the Gilded Age, with a continent full of seemingly unlimited natural resources and driven by millions of immigrants ready to work. In fact, some historians have referred to this era as America's second Industrial Revolution, because it completely changed American society, politics, and the economy. Mechanization and marketing were the keys to success in this age: companies that could mass-produce products and convince people to buy them accumulated enormous amounts of wealth, while companies that could not were forced out of business by brutal competition.

Railroads were the linchpin in the new industrialized economy. The railroad industry enabled raw materials, finished products, food, and people to travel cross-country in a matter of days, as opposed to the months or years that it took just prior to the Civil War. By the end of the war, the United States boasted some 35,000 miles of track, mostly in the industrialized North. By the turn of the century, that number had jumped to almost 200,000 miles, linking the North, South, and West. With these railroads making travel easier, millions of rural Americans flocked to the cities, and by 1900, nearly 40 percent of the population lived in urban areas.

By the twentieth century, the rise of big business and the large migration of Americans from the countryside to the cities caused a shift in political awareness, as elected officials saw the need to address the growing economic and social problems that developed along with the urban boom. So started the Progressive movement. Progressives believed that the government needed to take a strong, proactive role in the economy, regulating big business, immigration, and urban growth. These middle-class reformers hoped ultimately to regain control of the government from special interests like the railroads and trusts and pass effective legislation to protect consumers, organized labor, and minorities.

Summary of Events

Gilded Age Politics
Politics in the Gilded Age were intense. In the years between 1877 and 1897, control of the House of Representatives repeatedly changed hands between the Democratic and Republican parties. Political infighting between the **Stalwart** and **Half-Breed** factions in the Republican Party prevented the passage of significant legislation. During this era, the political parties nominated presidential candidates that lacked strong opinions—possibly to avoid stirring up sectional tensions so soon after the Civil War.

"The Forgotten Presidents"
Some historians have dubbed Presidents **Rutherford B. Hayes, James A. Garfield, Chester A. Arthur, Grover Cleveland**, and **Benjamin Harrison** the "forgotten presidents." Indeed, it might be argued that the most notable event that occurred during the Gilded Age was the assassination of President Garfield in 1881. His death prompted Congress to pass the **Pendleton Act,** which created the **Civil Service Commission** two years later. This commission reformed the **spoils system**, which had rewarded supporters of a winning party with "spoils," or posts in that party's government.

Industrialization and Big Business
The Civil War had transformed the North into one of the most heavily industrialized regions in the world, and during the Gilded Age, businessmen reaped enormous profits from this new economy. Powerful tycoons formed giant **trusts** to monopolize the production of goods that were in high demand. **Andrew Carnegie**, for one, built a giant steel empire using **vertical integration**, a business tactic that increased profits by eliminating middlemen from the production line. Conversely, **John D. Rockefeller**'s **Standard Oil Company** used **horizontal integration,** which put competitors out of business by selling one type of product in numerous markets, effectively creating a **monopoly**. These "captains of industry" cared little for consumers and did anything they could to increase profits, earning them the nickname **"robber barons."**

RAILROADS

Railroads were the literal engines behind this era of unprecedented industrial growth. By 1900, American railroad tycoons like **Cornelius Vanderbilt** had laid hundreds of thousands of miles of track across the country, transporting both tradable goods and passengers. The industry was hugely profitable for its leaders but riddled with corrupt practices, such as those associated with the **Crédit Mobilier** scandal of 1871. When the Supreme Court ruled in favor of corrupt railroads in the *Wabash* **case**, Congress passed the **Interstate Commerce Act** in 1887 to protect farmers and other consumers from unfair business practices.

ORGANIZED LABOR

Organized labor did not fare nearly as well as big business during the Gilded Age, as most Americans looked down on labor unions during the era. The first large-scale union, the **National Labor Union**, was formed just after the end of Civil War, in 1866. Workers created the union to protect skilled and unskilled workers in the countryside and in the cities, but the union collapsed after the **Depression of 1873** hit the United States. Later, the **Knights of Labor** represented skilled and unskilled workers, as well as blacks and women, in the 1870s, but it also folded after being wrongfully associated with the **Haymarket Square Bombing** in 1886.

Despite these setbacks for organized labor, workers continued to **strike**, or temporarily stop working, for better wages, hours, and working conditions. The most notable strikes of this era were the **Great Railroad Strike**, the **Homestead Strike**, and the **Pullman Strike**, all of which ended violently. The more exclusive **American Federation of Labor,** or AFL, emerged as the most powerful union in the late 1880s.

URBANIZATION AND IMMIGRATION

As profits soared, so did America's standard of living. During the latter half of the nineteenth century, millions of Americans left their farms and moved to the cities, which were filled with new wonders like skyscrapers, electric trolleys, and lightbulbs. Nearly a million eastern and southern European **immigrants** arrived in America each year, settling primarily in New York, Boston, Philadelphia, and Chicago. These new immigrants crowded into the poorest neighborhoods, the cities' crime- and disease-ridden **slums. Political machine** bosses like **William "Boss" Tweed** in New York preyed on immigrants, promising them public works projects and social services in exchange for their votes.

A growing middle class spurred a late-nineteenth-century reform movement to reduce poverty and improve society. Reformer **Jane Addams**, for example, founded **Hull House** in Chicago to help poor immigrant families adjust to life in America. The success of Hull House prompted other reformers to build similar **settlement houses** in the immigrant-clogged cities of the eastern United States.

THE WEST

The American West also underwent radical transformations. Railroads allowed more and more Americans to travel from overcrowded eastern cities and settle out West. Within a twenty-year period, American **settlers** had slaughtered more than 20 million bison, nearly causing the animal's extinction. Many **Native American tribes** of the West, including the Sioux, Fox, and Nez Percé, deeply resented white settlers' disregard for their land and primary food supply and began to attack the settlers. After a number of bloody battles, skirmishes, and massacres, the U.S. Army subdued the Native American population, herding them onto reservations. In an effort to **"Americanize"** Indians, Congress passed the **Dawes Severalty Act** in 1887, which forbade Native Americans from owning land.

THE POPULIST PARTY

The Depression of 1873, which effectively dissolved the National Labor Union, also threatened many new settlers in the Midwest. Plagued by steep railroad fares, high taxes under the **McKinley Tariff**, and soaring debt, thousands of small farmers banded together to form the **Populist Party** in the late 1880s. The Populists called for a national income tax, cheaper money (what Populists called **"free silver"**), shorter workdays, single-term limits for presidents, immigration restrictions, and government control of railroads.

CLEVELAND'S SECOND TERM

In 1892, **Grover Cleveland** defeated Republican incumbent **Benjamin Harrison** and Populist candidate **James B. Weaver** in 1892 to become the only U.S. president ever to serve two nonconsecutive terms. Although Cleveland's first four years were free of any major change, his second term was a tumultuous one. The **Depression of 1893** hit the U.S. economy hard, forcing Cleveland to ask Wall Street mogul **J. P. Morgan** for a loan of more than $60 million. In 1894, more than 500 protesters in **"Coxey's Army"** marched on Washington demanding cheaper money and debt relief. Despite Morgan's loan, Cleveland was unable to put the economy back on track, and it cost him the Republican Party presidential nomination in 1896.

THE ELECTION OF 1896

In 1896, Democrats nominated **William Jennings Bryan**, the "Boy Orator," after he delivered his famous **"Cross of Gold" speech** demanding free silver. Because Bryan incorporated much of the Populist platform into his own, the Populists chose to endorse him rather than their own candidate. Meanwhile, Republicans nominated Senator **William McKinley** from Ohio on a pro-business, anti–free silver platform. McKinley's campaign manager, **Marcus "Mark" Hanna**, worked behind the scenes to convince powerful business leaders to back several key Republican candidates. As a result, McKinley won the election of 1896, effectively killing free silver and the Populist movement.

THE SPANISH-AMERICAN WAR

McKinley's greatest challenge as president was the growing tension between the United States and Spain over the island of **Cuba**. Spanish officials had suppressed an independence movement in Cuba, its most profitable Caribbean colony, and forced Cuban men, women, and children into internment camps. **"Yellow journalists"** like **William Randolph Hearst** and **Joseph Pulitzer** published sensational stories about the atrocities in Cuba, partly to increase their papers' circulation but also to provoke American ire for the Spanish. Although McKinley did not want go to war, he felt compelled to do so, especially after the mysterious explosion of the **USS *Maine*** in Havana Harbor, which he blamed on Spain.

The war itself was over within a matter of weeks, but during that time, the United States seized the Philippines, Puerto Rico, and Cuba, thanks in part to future U.S. president **Theodore Roosevelt** and his **Rough Riders**. After the war, American forces withdrew from Cuba according to the **Teller Amendment** but also forced the new Cuban government to sign the **Platt Amendment**, giving the U.S. Navy a permanent military base at Guantánamo Bay, Cuba. The passage of the **Foraker Act**, meanwhile, granted Puerto Ricans limited government; they would not receive collective U.S. citizenship until 1917.

TEDDY ROOSEVELT'S BIG STICK POLICY

McKinley won the election of 1900 with Roosevelt as his running mate but was **assassinated** by an anarchist less than six months into his second term. As a result, Roosevelt took office as one of the youngest presidents in American history. Despite his youth, Roosevelt proved to be a "bully" with his **Big Stick diplomacy**. One of his most important policies, the **Roosevelt Corollary** to the Monroe Doctrine, declared that only the United States, not Old World powers, had the authority to interfere with Latin American affairs. Roosevelt's sec-retary of state, **John Hay**, drafted the **Open Door Notes**, which asked that Japan and the European powers respect China's territorial status and fair trade. Roosevelt went on to take over Colombia's northernmost province, Panama, in order to secure America the right to build the **Panama Canal**. Toward the end of his presidency, Roosevelt also toured with the **Great White Fleet**, a group of U.S. Navy battleships, around the world in a symbolic display of force.

ROOSEVELT AND PROGRESSIVISM
Roosevelt was just as active at home as he was abroad. During his presidency, America had become increasingly urbanized and industrialized. The **Progressive movement**, which formed as a response to the rapid social and economic growth and change that was taking place, helped spawn a new era of social reform. **Muckrakers**—journalists who wrote about political and industrial corruption as well as social hardships—had significant influence on Roosevelt, who outlined a package of domestic reforms called the **Square Deal**, which were meant to protect consumers, tame big business, support the labor movement, and conserve the nation's natural resources.

Congress, meanwhile, passed the **Elkins Act** and **Hepburn Act** to regulate the railroads and the **Pure Food and Drug Act** and **Meat Inspection Act** to regulate food inspection and sanitation. Congress passed the acts, in part, after the popularity of Upton Sinclair's novel *The Jungle*, which exposed unsanitary meatpacking practices. Roosevelt also supported strikers in the **Anthracite Strike**, prosecuted several trusts under the **Sherman Anti-Trust Act**, and signed the 1902 **Newlands Act**, selling lands in the West to fund irrigation projects.

TAFT'S PRESIDENCY
Roosevelt's friend and handpicked successor **William Howard Taft** promised to carry out the rest of Roosevelt's progressive policies if he were elected president. After winning the election of 1908, however, Taft proved to be more of a traditional conservative than most had expected. Although he continued progressive policy by prosecuting more trusts than his predecessor, in a more conservative vein

than Roosevelt he signed the steep **Payne-Aldrich Tariff** in 1909 and fired conservationist **Gifford Pinchot** from the forestry division. Many Republican Progressives, including his former friend Roosevelt, denounced Taft as a traitor to the movement. When Republicans nominated Taft again in 1912, Roosevelt left the convention and entered the presidential race as the candidate for the new **Progressive Republican** or **Bull Moose Party**.

WILSON'S FIRST TERM

With two feuding party leaders splitting the Republican vote, Democrat **Woodrow Wilson** managed to win the presidential election. Also a Progressive, Wilson championed a new group of reforms, the **New Freedom**, which regulated big business, further supported the labor movement, and reduced tariffs. In 1913, he signed the **Underwood Tariff**, which was lower than Taft's, and also reformed the national banking system with the **Federal Reserve Act**. The following year, Wilson passed the **Clayton Anti-Trust Act** to replace the much weaker Sherman Act of 1890, which was riddled with loopholes. Other progressive bills he signed into law included the **Warehouse Act**, the **La Follette Seaman's Act**, the **Workingman's Compensation Act**, and the **Adamson Act**. Wilson also ordered General **John "Blackjack" Pershing** to invade Mexico in 1916 to pursue the bandit **Pancho Villa**.

SUMMARY OF EVENTS

KEY PEOPLE & TERMS

PEOPLE

JANE ADDAMS
Social activist who founded **Hull House** in Chicago in 1889 to help immigrants improve their lives in the city's slums. Addams won the Nobel Prize for Peace for her efforts, which raised awareness of the plight of the poor and opened up new opportunities for the advancement of American women.

CHESTER A. ARTHUR
Vice president under **James A. Garfield** who became the twenty-first U.S. president in September 1881 after Garfield was assassinated. As president, Arthur refused to award **Stalwarts** federal posts and helped legislate civil service reform by signing the **Pendleton Act** in 1883.

WILLIAM JENNINGS BRYAN
Nebraska congressman who gave the famous **"Cross of Gold" speech** and was the Democratic Party nominee for president in the election of 1896. Known as the "Boy Orator," Bryan was the greatest champion of inflationary **"free silver"** around the turn of the century. Although he never left the Democratic Party, he was closely affiliated with the grassroots **Populist movement**. The **Populist Party** later chose to back him in the election of 1900. Bryan ran for president in 1896, 1900, and 1908 but lost every time.

ANDREW CARNEGIE
Scottish immigrant who built a steel empire in Pittsburgh through hard work and ruthless business tactics such as **vertical integration**. Carnegie hated organized labor and sent in 300 Pinkerton agents to end the 1892 **Homestead Strike** at one of his steel plants. He eventually sold his company to Wall Street financier **J. P. Morgan**, who used it to form the **U.S. Steel Corporation** trust in 1901. Around the turn of the century, Carnegie became one of the nation's first large-scale **philanthropists** by donating more than $300 million to charities, hospitals, libraries, and universities.

GROVER CLEVELAND

Former Democratic governor of New York and both the twenty-second and twenty-fourth U.S. president—the only U.S. president ever elected to two nonconsecutive terms. During his rocky second term, Cleveland unsuccessfully battled the **Depression of 1893**, sent federal troops to break up the **Pullman Strike** in 1894, and had to ask **J. P. Morgan** to loan the nearly bankrupt federal government more than $60 million in 1895. Cleveland's inability to end the depression helped give rise to the **Populist movement** in the mid-1890s.

EUGENE V. DEBS

Labor supporter who helped organize the **Pullman Strike** in 1894. Debs later formed the **Socialist Party** in the early 1900s and ran unsuccessfully for the presidency in 1908 against William Howard Taft and William Jennings Bryan.

JAMES A. GARFIELD

Twentieth U.S. president, elected in 1880, who spent less than a year in office before he was assassinated. The assassin was a Republican Stalwart who wanted Garfield's vice president, **Chester A. Arthur**, to become president. Garfield's death compelled Congress to pass the **Pendleton Act** in 1883 to reform civil service.

BENJAMIN HARRISON

Twenty-third U.S. president, elected in 1888, and the grandson of ninth U.S. president William Henry Harrison.

WILLIAM McKINLEY

Powerful Ohio congressman and twenty-fifth U.S. president. As a member of Congress, McKinley managed to pass the **McKinley Tariff** in 1890, which raised the protective tariff rates on foreign goods to an all-time high. In 1896, he ran for president on a pro–**gold standard** platform against Democrat William Jennings Bryan; McKinley's campaign manager, **Mark Hanna**, and wealthy plutocrats ensured that McKinley won the presidency. Although McKinley personally opposed the **Spanish-American War**, he asked Congress to declare war against Spain in 1898, fearing that the Democrats would unseat him in the next presidential election. He signed the **Gold Standard Act** in 1900 and was reelected later that year, but an anarchist assassinated him in 1901.

J. P. MORGAN
A wealthy Wall Street banker who saved the nearly bankrupt federal government in 1895 by loaning the Treasury more than $60 million. Morgan later purchased **Andrew Carnegie**'s steel company for nearly $400 million and used it to form the **U.S. Steel Corporation** in 1901.

JOHN D. ROCKEFELLER
Industrialist who founded the **Standard Oil Company** in 1870. An incredibly ruthless businessman, Rockefeller employed **horizontal integration** to make Standard Oil one of the nation's first monopolistic trusts.

THEODORE ROOSEVELT
Twenty-sixth U.S. president, who took office after the assassination of **William McKinley** in 1901. Roosevelt, already famous for his aggressive policies, continued them as president both at home and abroad. His domestic policies, collectively known as the **Square Deal**, sought to protect American consumers, regulate big business, conserve natural resources, and help organized labor. His **Roosevelt corollary** to the Monroe Doctrine asserted American influence and power in Latin America. Although Roosevelt endorsed **William Howard Taft** in 1908, he split the Republican Party by running against Taft in 1912 on the **Progressive Party**, or **Bull Moose Party**, ticket.

WILLIAM HOWARD TAFT
Theodore Roosevelt's handpicked successor and the twenty-seventh U.S. president. Taft, elected in 1908 on a Progressive platform, ultimately alienated himself from his fellow Republicans by supporting the **Payne-Aldrich Tariff** and firing conservationist **Gifford Pinchot**. He and Roosevelt split the Republican Party in the election of 1912, giving Democrat **Woodrow Wilson** an easy victory.

CORNELIUS VANDERBILT
A wealthy, corrupt **railroad** tycoon and innovator. Vanderbilt was one of the first in the industry to make rails out of **steel** instead of iron and also established a standard gauge for his railroads. Despite these innovations that led to the improvement of the railroad industry, he and his son were notorious **"robber barons"** who issued unfair rebates, hiked rates arbitrarily, and cared little for American consumers.

WOODROW WILSON

Twenty-eighth U.S. president of the United States. Wilson entered the White House in 1913 after defeating Republican incumbent **William Howard Taft** and former president **Theodore Roosevelt**. Wilson's **New Freedom** domestic policies called for lowering the protective tariff and taming big business. (*For information on Wilson and U.S. involvement in World War I, see the History SparkNote* World War I.)

TERMS

AMERICAN FEDERATION OF LABOR (AFL)

An umbrella organization for smaller independent unions founded and headed by labor organizer **Samuel Gompers**. The AFL protected only skilled workers and had a limited membership of a half a million workers around the turn of the century. It fought businesses for higher wages, shorter workdays, and improvements in the work environment.

"CROSS OF GOLD" SPEECH

Speech delivered by **William Jennings Bryan** at the Democratic presidential nominating convention in 1896. In the speech, Bryan railed against the **gold standard** and proposed to issue paper money that would be backed by **silver**. Though he lost the election, his speech is regarded as one of the finest speeches ever delivered in American politics.

DEPRESSION OF 1893

A depression caused by overspeculation, depressed agricultural prices, and weakened American credit abroad. The worst depression in America since the 1870s, the Depression of 1893 hit farmers hard and left millions in the cities without work. President **Grover Cleveland**'s inability to end the depression caused social unrest and helped strengthen the **Populist Party**'s following.

GOSPEL OF WEALTH

A social doctrine espoused by many wealthy businessmen during the Gilded Age that justified the growing income gap between rich and poor by arguing that God blessed the industrious with riches.

HALF-BREEDS

A faction within the Republican Party during the 1870s and 1880s that exploited the spoils system. The Half-Breeds, led by congressman **James G. Blaine** of Maine, engaged in a rivalry with the **Stalwarts** that weakened the Republican Party and ultimately played a part in the assassination of President **James A. Garfield**.

HAYMARKET SQUARE BOMBING

An explosion in the middle of a labor strike in Chicago's **Haymarket Square** in 1886. Although investigators later concluded that anarchists had detonated the bomb, the American people quickly placed blame on the strikers. The bombing brought an end to the union group the **Knights of Labor**.

HORIZONTAL INTEGRATION

A business tactic, often employed by Gilded Age businessmen, that seeks to put competitors out of business by selling one type of product in various markets. Another way to accomplish horizontal integration is to buy these competing companies and limit consumer access to a particular commodity, thereby creating a **monopoly**.

HULL HOUSE

A social settlement founded by **Jane Addams** in the slums of Chicago in 1889. Hull House attempted to improve life for the city's impoverished immigrants by offering them classes, counseling, and day-care services.

INTERSTATE COMMERCE ACT

A bill passed in 1887 to restrict corrupt practices in the **railroad industry**. The act outlawed uncompetitive rebates and forced railroad companies to publish their prices outright. Congress passed the bill in the wake of the Supreme Court's ruling in the **Wabash** case. The act also created the **Interstate Commerce Commission** (ICC) to ensure that the railroad companies adhered to the new law.

KNIGHTS OF LABOR

An all-inclusive union founded in 1869 for skilled and unskilled American laborers, men and women, black and white. The Knights of Labor replaced the **National Labor Union**. When the union was falsely implicated in the 1886 **Haymarket Square Bombing** in Chicago, it ended up losing thousands of its members.

USS MAINE

A U.S. Navy ship that exploded mysteriously in the harbor of Havana, **Cuba**, in 1898. Although historians have since concluded that a boiler accident caused the ship to explode, **yellow journalists** published sensationalist stories about the incident that quickly led the American public to believe that agents from **Spain** had sabotaged the ship. The destruction of the *Maine* pushed the United States and Spain closer to the **Spanish-American War**.

McKinley Tariff

A bill passed in 1890 that was one of the highest tariffs in U.S. history, increasing the tax on foreign goods to approximately 50 percent. The tariff was highly unpopular among farmers in the Midwest and South, who over the next few years voted out many Republicans who had supported the bill, including President **Benjamin Harrison**. The tariff's unpopularity also helped widen the influence of the **Populist Party**.

Muckrakers

Exposé writers who informed the public about many corporate evils and social injustices in the late nineteenth and early twentieth centuries. Many muckraker articles and books, such as Upton Sinclair's novel *The Jungle*, pushed the U.S. government to launch reform campaigns and contributed to the **Progressive movement**.

New Freedom

President **Woodrow Wilson**'s comprehensive package of domestic policies that sought to lower tariffs, regulate trusts, and protect organized labor.

Open Door Notes

A group of notes sent by Secretary of State **John Hay** to Japan and several European powers, requesting that they respect Chinese rights and the policy of free trade. Hay sent the **First Open Door Note** in 1899, fearing that the United States would be excluded from lucrative trade rights in Asia. He drafted the **Second Open Door Note** in 1900, partly to ensure that the major European powers would recognize China's territorial integrity, and partly because he feared that Europe would use the violence of the 1900 **Boxer Rebellion** as a justification for colonizing China.

Pendleton Act

Bill passed after President **James A. Garfield**'s assassination in 1881 that created the **Civil Service Commission**. The commission administered competitive examinations to civil service workers to reform the **spoils system**.

Populist Party

Political party founded in 1891 by farmers in the Midwest who were suffering from the ill effects of high, pro–big-business tariffs. The Populists campaigned for **shorter workdays**, **nationalization** of public utilities, **direct election** of senators, the recall and **referendum**, a one-term limit for presidents, and cheap paper money backed by **silver** (at a ratio of sixteen ounces of silver to one ounce of gold). Although William Jennings Bryan's loss in the election of 1896 broke up the party, Populist ideals endured and later coalesced into the **Progressive movement**.

Roosevelt Corollary to the Monroe Doctrine

President **Theodore Roosevelt**'s addendum to the **Monroe Doctrine**, which effectively declared that only the United States could intervene in the affairs of **Latin America**. Roosevelt made the declaration in 1904 to prevent Britain, Germany, Italy, and other European nations from forcibly collecting unpaid debts in Latin America.

Sherman Anti-Trust Act

A bill passed by Congress in 1890 that was intended to ban big business **monopolies**. Ironically, lawmakers used the Sherman Anti-Trust Act to prosecute more **labor unions** than corporate monopolies during the 1890s. Roosevelt and Taft later used the act to prosecute dozens of trusts like **Standard Oil** and the **U.S. Steel Corporation**. In 1914, the tougher **Clayton Anti-Trust Act** replaced the Sherman Act, eliminating many of the older act's loopholes.

Social Darwinism

The application of **Charles Darwin**'s theories of natural selection to a business-oriented society. Beginning in the 1880s, a growing number of scholars and business leaders began to view social problems through the lens of Darwin's theories. These **Social Darwinists** argued that the new self-made captains of industry were wealthy because they had proven themselves to be the best among men. Conversely, the theory also implied that the poor remained poor because of their own inferiority.

Square Deal

The collective term for **Theodore Roosevelt**'s set of progressive domestic policies, which aimed to regulate big business, help organized labor, protect consumers, and conserve the country's dwindling natural resources.

KEY PEOPLE & TERMS

STALWARTS

A faction within the Republican Party during the 1870s and 1880s that exploited the **spoils system**. The leader of the Stalwart faction was Senator **Roscoe Conkling** of New York. The Stalwarts' rivalry with the **Half-Breeds**, another Republican faction during this time period, weakened the Republican Party significantly.

VERTICAL INTEGRATION

A business strategy, often used by Gilded Age tycoons, that attempts to insulate a company from competition by integrating every aspect of production into a single company, thus eliminating middlemen. Steel baron **Andrew Carnegie**, for example, owned coal and iron fields, railroads, shipping companies, and marketing interests that were involved in the transportation and sale of his steel. By eliminating expensive middlemen, businessmen like Carnegie could secure more profit for themselves.

WABASH CASE

An 1886 Supreme Court ruling that declared that only the federal government could regulate interstate commerce. The case prompted Congress to pass the **Interstate Commerce Act** a year later.

SUMMARY & ANALYSIS

GILDED AGE POLITICS: 1877–1892

EVENTS

1876	Rutherford B. Hayes is elected president
1877	Railroad workers strike across United States
1880	James A. Garfield is elected president
1881	Garfield is assassinated; Chester A. Arthur becomes president
1883	Congress passes Pendleton Act
1884	Grover Cleveland is elected president
1888	Benjamin Harrison is elected president
1890	Congress passes Sherman Silver Purchase Act, Pension Act, and McKinley Tariff

KEY PEOPLE

Rutherford B. Hayes 19th U.S. president; technically lost election but took office after Compromise of 1877 with Democrats

James A. Garfield 20th U.S. president; elected in 1880 but assassinated after less than a year in office

Chester A. Arthur 21st U.S. president; took office in 1881 after Garfield's assassination

James G. Blaine Congressman from Maine; leader of Half-Breeds in the Republican Party

Grover Cleveland 22nd and 24th U.S. president; first elected in 1884 after defeating James G. Blaine

Roscoe Conkling New York senator; leader of the Stalwarts in the Republican Party

Benjamin Harrison 23rd U.S. president and grandson of ninth U.S. president, William Henry Harrison; defeated incumbent Grover Cleveland in 1888

William "Boss" Tweed Corrupt Democrat who controlled most of New York City politics during the Gilded Age

HAYES

Rutherford B. Hayes had little political power during his four years in office, having barely squeaked into the White House by one vote after the **Compromise of 1877**, in which the Democrats ceded the White House to the Republicans in exchange for an end to **Reconstruction** in the South. The real winners in the election were Republican **spoils seekers** who flooded Washington, D.C., in search of civil service jobs.

STALWARTS AND HALF-BREEDS

Disputes over these spoils split the Republican Party into two factions: the **Stalwarts**, led by Senator **Roscoe Conkling** of New York, and the **Half-Breeds**, led by Congressman **James G. Blaine** of Maine.

Neither group trusted the other, and the split left the Republican Party unable to pass any significant legislation during this time.

THE RAILROAD STRIKE OF 1877

The only major upheaval during Hayes's presidency was the **Great Railroad Strike** of 1877, when railroad workers throughout the United States went on strike to protest the lowering of their salaries. More than a hundred people died during violence related to the strike, forcing Hayes to use federal troops to suppress the uprisings.

THE ELECTION OF 1880

By the election of 1880, the Republicans, no longer supporting Rutherford B. Hayes, nominated the relatively unknown Ohioan **James A. Garfield** for president, along with the Stalwart running mate **Chester A. Arthur**. Democrats nominated Civil War veteran **Winfield Scott Hancock**, and the pro-labor **Greenback Party** nominated **James B. Weaver**. In the election, Garfield received a sizable majority of electoral votes but won the popular vote by only a slim margin over Hancock.

GARFIELD AND HAYES

Like Hayes's, Garfield's presidency was overshadowed by Stalwart and Half-Breed infighting. In the summer of 1881, Garfield's term was cut short when a delusional Stalwart supporter named **Charles Guiteau** assassinated Garfield in Washington, D.C. Guiteau hoped that Vice President Arthur would become president and give more federal jobs to Stalwarts.

Although Arthur did replace Garfield, the assassination convinced policymakers that the U.S. government was in dire need of **civil service reform** to combat the spoils system. Congress therefore passed the **Pendleton Act** in 1883, which created the **Civil Service Commission** to ensure that hiring of federal employees was based on examinations and merit rather than political patronage.

THE ELECTION OF 1884

The election of 1884 was one of the most contentious in U.S. history. The spoils system remained the central issue of the political contest, and candidates debated about what it would take to reform civil service. Republicans nominated Half-Breed **James Blaine** of Maine, while Democrats nominated Governor **Grover Cleveland** of New York. The Democratic Party accused Blaine of conspiring with wealthy plutocrats to win the White House, while Republicans attacked Cleveland for having an illegitimate son. In the end, Cleveland barely defeated Blaine, by a margin of only forty electoral votes and a paltry 30,000 popular votes.

Cleveland and Harrison

Cleveland's first four years were fairly uneventful; his only major action was his proposal of a lower tariff to reduce the Treasury surplus near the end of his term. When the election of 1888 rolled around, Republicans rallied big business in the North and nominated **Benjamin Harrison**, a grandson of ninth U.S. president William Henry Harrison. Republicans were afraid that Democrats would succeed in lowering the protective tariff, so Harrison campaigned for an even higher tariff. Democrats countered by renominating Grover Cleveland. The results of the election were just as close as the other presidential elections of the Gilded Age, and Harrison ended up victorious.

During Harrison's term, the Republican-majority Congress passed several notable bills, including the **Sherman Silver Purchase Act**, which allowed the government to buy more silver to produce currency; the **Pension Act**, which distributed more money to Civil War veterans; and the controversial **McKinley Tariff**, which increased duties on foreign goods to about 50 percent.

INDUSTRIALIZATION: 1869–1901

EVENTS

1869	Transcontinental Railroad is completed
1870	Standard Oil Company forms
1886	Supreme Court issues verdict in *Wabash* case
1887	Congress passes Interstate Commerce Act
1890	Congress passes Sherman Anti-Trust Act
1901	U.S. Steel Corporation forms

KEY PEOPLE

Andrew Carnegie Scottish-American business tycoon and owner of the Carnegie Steel Company in Pittsburgh; used vertical integration to maintain market dominance

John D. Rockefeller Founder of the Standard Oil Company; used horizontal integration to effectively buy out his competition

Cornelius Vanderbilt Steamboat and railroad tycoon; laid thousands of miles of railroad track and established standard gauge for railroads

SUMMARY & ANALYSIS

TRANSCONTINENTAL RAILROADS

Gilded Age **industrialization** had its roots in the Civil War, which spurred Congress and the northern states to build more **railroads** and increased demand for a variety of **manufactured goods**. The forward-looking Congress of 1862 authorized construction of the first **transcontinental railroad**, connecting the Pacific and Atlantic lines. Originally, because railroading was such an expensive enterprise at the time, the federal government provided subsidies by the mile to railroad companies in exchange for discounted rates. Congress also provided federal land grants to railroad companies so that they could lay down more track.

With this free land and tens of thousands of dollars per mile in subsidies, railroading became a highly profitable business venture. The **Union Pacific Railroad** company began construction on the transcontinental line in Nebraska during the Civil War and pushed westward, while **Leland Stanford**'s **Central Pacific Railroad** pushed eastward from Sacramento. Tens of thousands of Irish and Chinese laborers laid the track, and the two lines finally met near Promontory, Utah, in 1869.

CAPTAINS OF INDUSTRY

Big businessmen, not politicians, controlled the new industrialized America of the Gilded Age. Whereas past generations sent their best men into public service, in the last decades of the 1800s, young men were enticed by the private sector, where with a little persistence, hard work, and ruthlessness, one could reap enormous profits. These so-called **"captains of industry"** were not regulated by the government and did whatever they could to make as much money as possible. These industrialists' business practices were sometimes so unscrupulous that they were given the name **"robber barons."**

VANDERBILT AND THE RAILROADS
As the railroad boom accelerated, railroads began to crisscross the West. Some of the major companies included the **Southern Pacific Railroad**, the **Santa Fe Railroad**, and the **North Pacific Railroad**. Federal subsidies and land grants made railroading such a profitable business that a class of "new money" millionaires emerged.

Cornelius Vanderbilt and his son William were perhaps the most famous railroad tycoons. During the era, they bought out and consolidated many of the rail companies in the East, enabling them to cut operations costs. The Vanderbilts also established a standard **track gauge** and were among the first railroaders to replace iron rails with lighter, more durable steel. The Vanderbilt fortune swelled to more than $100 million during these boom years.

RAILROAD CORRUPTION
As the railroad industry grew, it became filled with corrupt practices. Unhindered by government regulation, railroaders could turn enormous profits using any method to get results, however unethical. Union Pacific officials, for example, formed the dummy **Crédit Mobilier** construction company and hired themselves out as contractors at enormous rates for huge profits. Several U.S. congressmen were implicated in the scandal after an investigation uncovered that the company bribed them to keep quiet about the corruption. Railroads also inflated the prices of their stocks and gave out noncompetitive rebates to favored companies.

Moreover, tycoons such as the Vanderbilts were notorious for their lack of regard for the common worker. Although some states passed laws to regulate corrupt railroads, the Supreme Court made regulation on a state level impossible with the 1886 *Wabash* **case** ruling, which stated that only the federal government could regulate interstate commerce.

CARNEGIE, MORGAN, AND U.S. STEEL
Among the wealthiest and most famous captains of industry in the late 1800s was **Andrew Carnegie**. A Scottish immigrant, Carnegie turned his one Pennsylvanian production plant into a veritable **steel**

empire through a business tactic called **vertical integration**. Rather than rely on expensive middlemen, Carnegie vertically integrated his production process by buying out all of the companies—coal, iron ore, and so on—needed to produce his steel, as well as the companies that produced the steel, shipped it, and sold it. Eventually, Carnegie sold his company to banker **J. P. Morgan**, who used the company as the foundation for the **U.S. Steel Corporation**. By the end of his life, Carnegie was one of the richest men in America, with a fortune of nearly $500 million.

ROCKEFELLER AND STANDARD OIL

Oil was another lucrative business during the Gilded Age. Although there was very little need for oil prior to the Civil War, demand surged during the machine age of the 1880s, 1890s, and early 1900s. Seemingly everything required oil during this era: factory machines, ships, and, later, automobiles.

The biggest names in the oil industry were **John D. Rockefeller** and his **Standard Oil Company**—in fact, they were the *only* names in the industry. Whereas Carnegie employed vertical integration to create his steel empire, Rockefeller used **horizontal integration**, essentially buying out all the other oil companies so that he had no competition left. In doing so, Rockefeller created one of America's first **monopolies**, or **trusts**, that cornered the market of a single product.

SOCIAL DARWINISM AND THE GOSPEL OF WEALTH

In time, many wealthy American businessmen, inspired by biologist **Charles Darwin**'s new theories of natural selection, began to believe that they had become rich because they were literally superior human beings compared to the poorer classes. The wealthy applied Darwin's idea of "survival of the fittest" to society; in the words of one **Social Darwinist**, as they became known, "The millionaires are the product of natural selection." Pious plutocrats preached the **"Gospel of Wealth,"** which was similar to Social Darwinism but explained a person's great riches as a gift from God

REGULATING BIG BUSINESS

Without any form of government regulation, big business owners were able to create **monopolies**—companies that control all aspects of production for certain products. Economists agree that monopolies are rarely good for the market, as they often stifle competition, inflate prices, and hurt consumers.

In the late 1880s and early 1890s, the U.S. government stepped in and tried to start regulating the growing number of monopolies. In 1887, Congress passed the **Interstate Commerce Act**, which outlawed railroad rebates and kickbacks and also established the **Interstate Commerce Commission** to ensure that the railroad companies obeyed the new laws. The bill was riddled with loopholes, however, and had very little effect. In 1890, Congress also passed the **Sherman Anti-Trust Act** in an attempt to ban trusts, but this, too, was an ineffective piece of legislation and was replaced with revised legislation in the early 1900s.

THE LABOR MOVEMENT: 1866–1894

EVENTS

1866	National Labor Union forms
1869	Knights of Labor forms
1877	Railroad workers strike nationwide
1886	Haymarket Square bombing American Federation of Labor forms
1892	Miners strike in Coeur d'Alene, Idaho Homestead Strike occurs
1894	Pullman Strike occurs

KEY PEOPLE

Eugene V. Debs Labor leader who helped organize Pullman Strike; later became socialist leader and presidential candidate

Samuel Gompers Union leader; founded American Federation of Labor (AFL) in 1886 to represent skilled urban craftsmen

THE NATIONAL LABOR UNION

The first large-scale U.S. union was the **National Labor Union**, founded in 1866 to organize skilled and unskilled laborers, farmers, and factory workers. Blacks and women, however, were not allowed to join the union. Though the National Labor Union was not affiliated with any particular political party, it generally supported any candidate who would fight for shorter workdays, higher wages, and better working conditions.

The National Labor Union existed for only six years. When the **Depression of 1873** hit, workers' rights were put on hold; Americans needed *any* wages, not better wages. Moreover, union members found it difficult to engage in collective bargaining with company heads when companies could easily hire thousands of immigrant "scabs," or strikebreakers.

THE KNIGHTS OF LABOR

The **Knights of Labor**, however, survived the depression. Originally a secret society in 1869, the Knights picked up where the National Labor Union had left off. The union united skilled and unskilled laborers in the countryside and cities in one group. Unlike the National Labor Union, the Knights allowed blacks and women among its ranks. Although they did win a series of strikes in their fight against long hours and low wages, they generally had difficulty bargaining collectively because they represented such a diverse group of workers. The Knights did not exist for very long: when members were falsely associated with the anarchists who were responsible for the **Haymarket Square Bombing** in Chicago in 1886, the union fell apart soon thereafter.

THE HOMESTEAD STRIKE

Several major labor strikes occurred in the early 1890s, foremost among them the **Homestead Strike**, which protested wage cuts at one of **Andrew Carnegie**'s steel plants in Pittsburgh, Pennsylvania. When Pittsburgh police refused to end the strike, Carnegie hired 300 private agents from the renowned **Pinkerton Detective Agency** to subdue the protest. The laborers, however, won a surprising victory after a bloody standoff. President **Benjamin Harrison** eventually sent troops to end the strike.

THE PULLMAN STRIKE

In 1894, reelected president **Grover Cleveland** made a decision similar to Harrison's to end the **Pullman Strike** in Chicago. When Pullman, a railroad car company, cut employees' wages by 30 percent, labor organizer **Eugene V. Debs** organized a massive strike. Over 150,000 Pullman workers refused to work, Pullman cars were destroyed, and train service was cut off from Chicago to California. Cleveland sent federal troops to break up the strike and had them arrest its ringleader, Debs.

THE AMERICAN FEDERATION OF LABOR

During these turbulent years for America's labor unions, the **American Federation of Labor** (AFL) quietly grew in power, coordinating efforts for several dozen independent labor unions. **Samuel Gompers** founded the union in 1886, seeking better wages, working conditions, shorter working days, and the creation of all-union workplaces for its members. Unlike the National Labor Union and the Knights of Labor, the AFL represented only skilled white male craftsmen in the cities. Despite this limitation, however, the AFL survived the Gilded Age and would become one of the most powerful labor unions in the new century.

SUMMARY & ANALYSIS

GILDED AGE SOCIETY: 1870–1900

EVENTS

1876	Alexander Graham Bell invents telephone
1879	Thomas Edison invents lightbulb
1881	Booker T. Washington becomes president of Tuskegee Institute
1882	Congress passes Chinese Exclusion Act
1889	Jane Addams founds Hull House in Chicago
1893	Lillian Wald founds Henry Street Settlement in New York
1896	Supreme Court issues *Plessy v. Ferguson* ruling

KEY PEOPLE

Jane Addams Social activist; founded Hull House in 1889 to assist poor Chicago immigrants

W. E. B. Du Bois Black historian and sociologist; lobbied for equal economic and social rights for African Americans

Booker T. Washington President of Tuskegee Institute, the first major black industrial college; believed that economic equality would bring equal rights for blacks

URBANIZATION

The Gilded Age saw the United States shift from an agricultural to an urban, industrial society, as millions of Americans flocked to **cities** in the post–Civil War era. Nearly 40 percent of Americans lived in urbanized areas by 1900, as opposed to 20 percent in 1860. Many young people left the countryside in search of new wonders: cities were at the height of modernization for the time, with skyscrapers, electric trolleys, department stores, bridges, bicycles, indoor plumbing, telephones, and electric lamps. Industrialization and the rush to the cities led to the development of **consumerism** and a **middle class**.

MASS IMMIGRATION

In addition to this major shift from rural to urban areas, a new wave of **immigration** increased America's population significantly, especially in major cities. Immigrants came from war-torn regions of **southern and eastern Europe**, such as Italy, Greece, Poland, Russia, Croatia, and Czechoslovakia. This new group of immigrants was poorer and less educated than the Irish and German immigrants who had made the journey to the United States earlier in the century. By the early twentieth century, more than a million immigrants were entering eastern U.S. cities on a yearly basis. Many immigrants could barely make a living, working as unskilled laborers in factories or packinghouses for low wages.

NATIVISM

Many **nativists**—Americans descended primarily from Irish and German immigrants (but not exclusively those groups)—claimed that the newly arriving southern and eastern European immigrants would not be able to assimilate into American society. They saw these immigrants as illiterate and poor, unable to learn English and with little experience living in a democratic society. Many of America's Protestants also disliked the fact that many of the new immigrants were Catholic, Eastern Orthodox, or Jewish. Many Anglo-Saxon Americans worried that eastern and southern Europeans would "outbreed" them and take over their once-"pure" race. Many nativists joined the **American Protective Association** to lobby for immigration restrictions; Congress conceded and eventually barred criminals and the extremely destitute from entry in 1882.

Nativists in the United States reserved special hatred for **Chinese** immigrants—a group that had worked countless hours of labor at low wages, especially on railroad construction in the West. Unions pressed Congress to pass the **Chinese Exclusion Act** in 1882, completely banning Chinese immigration to the United States. Congress did pass the act, and it remained in place until 1943.

URBAN SLUMS

The sudden influx of millions of poor immigrants led to the formation of slums in U.S. cities. These new city dwellers lived in **tenement** buildings, often with entire families living together in tiny one-room apartments and sharing a single bathroom with other families on the floor. Tenements generally were filthy, poorly ventilated, and poorly lit, making them a hospitable environment for rats and disease.

JANE ADDAMS AND HULL HOUSE

A social reform movement emerged as a result of these worsening living and working conditions in America's cities. Foremost among the reformers was **Jane Addams**, a college-educated woman who founded **Hull House** in 1889 in one of Chicago's poorest neighborhoods. Hull House provided counseling, day-care services, and adult education classes to help local immigrants.

The success of Hull House prompted **Lillian Wald** to open the **Henry Street Settlement House** in New York in 1893. The combined success of these settlement houses prompted other reformers to open similar houses in other eastern cities with large immigrant populations. In time, women like Addams and Wald used their positions of power to fight for women's suffrage, temperance, civil rights, and improved labor laws.

BLACK CIVIL RIGHTS

In 1896, the Supreme Court upheld the policy of segregation by legalizing **"separate but equal"** facilities for blacks and whites in the landmark *Plessy v. Ferguson* decision. In doing so, the court condemned blacks to more than another half century of second-class citizenship.

Despite the ruling, African-American leaders of the **civil rights movement** continued to press for equal rights. **Booker T. Washington**, president of the all-black **Tuskegee Institute** in Alabama, rather than press for immediate social equality, encouraged blacks to become economically self-sufficient so that they could challenge whites on social issues in the future. The Harvard-educated black historian and sociologist **W. E. B. Du Bois**, on the other hand, ridiculed Washington's beliefs and argued that blacks should fight for immediate—and overdue—social and economic equality. This dispute between Washington and Du Bois encapsulated the divide in the civil rights movement at the end of the nineteenth century and the question as to how blacks could most effectively pursue equality—a debate that lasted well into the civil rights movement of the 1960s and continues today.

THE WEST: 1860–1900

EVENTS

1862	Congress passes Homestead Act
1864	Sand Creek Massacre
1867	National Grange forms
1869	First transcontinental railroad is completed
1875	Sioux Wars occur in Dakota Territory
1876	Battle of Little Bighorn
1877	Nez Percé War
1885	Farmers' Alliance forms
1887	Congress passes Dawes Severalty Act
1890	U.S. Census Bureau declares frontier closed Battle of Wounded Knee
1891	Populist Party forms
1893	Turner publishes *The Significance of the Frontier in American History*

KEY PEOPLE

Chief Joseph Nez Percé chief in the Pacific Northwest; opposed white expansion westward and relocation to reservations; captured by U.S. forces in 1877

Geronimo Apache chief who led a rebellion against white American settlement of the Southwest in the 1870s and 1880s

Sitting Bull Sioux chief who helped defeat General George Custer at the Battle of Little Bighorn in 1876

Frederick Jackson Turner Historian whose 1893 essay *The Significance of the Frontier in American History* argued that western settlement had had an extraordinary impact on U.S. social, political, and economic development

RAILROADS AND THE WEST

More than any other single factor, **railroads** transformed the industrial cities of the West during the late 1800s. Railroads made travel easier, cheaper, and safer. The long **transcontinental lines** moved people, grain, cattle, ore, and equipment back and forth across the vast expanses of the Midwest, over the Rocky Mountains, Sierra Nevada, and to the fertile valleys of California and Oregon.

Railroads also transformed the western landscape. For millennia, millions of **bison** had roamed the Great Plains of the Midwest, providing food and clothing for Native American tribes. Even by the end of the Civil War, there were still as many as 20 million bison west of the Mississippi. The railroads, however, destroyed the bison's natural environment, and worse, transported sport hunters to the region. Americans slaughtered so many bison in their trek westward that by 1885, only about 1,000 remained.

THE HOMESTEAD ACT

Americans continued to move westward even during the turmoil of the Civil War. After the war ended, several million Americans immigrated to the regions beyond eastern Kansas and Nebraska, enticed by cheap federal land that Congress offered in the **Homestead Act** of 1862. Under the act, any individual settler paying a small filing fee could stake a claim to 160 acres of free land in the West, as long as his family "improved" the land by farming it and living on it.

THE INDIAN WARS

As white settlers pushed farther westward and repeatedly drove Native Americans from their lands, clashes between tribes and settlers became inevitable. In 1864, Union troops killed several hundred Indian women and children at the **Sand Creek Massacre** in Colorado. The U.S. Army also fought the **Sioux Wars** in the Black Hills of the Dakota Territory during the 1860s and 1870s. In 1876, General **George Armstrong Custer** made his infamous last stand during the **Battle of Little Bighorn**, when all 264 of his troops fell at the hands of Chief **Sitting Bull** and his warriors. The Sioux's victory was short-lived, however, as the tribe was defeated a year later.

In addition, the U.S. Army fought the **Nez Percé** tribe in the Pacific Northwest when the tribe's leader, **Chief Joseph**, refused to relinquish the Nez Percé's lands to white settlers. They were eventually defeated and resettled in Kansas. In the New Mexico Territory, the **Apache** tribe, led by **Geronimo**, fought bravely to protect their homelands but were eventually defeated and relocated to Oklahoma and rural areas of the South. Hundreds of Native Americans also died at the **Battle of Wounded Knee** in 1890, during the army's attempt to end the **Ghost Dance Movement**—a Native American movement that called for a return to traditional ways of life and challenged white dominance in society.

THE DAWES SEVERALTY ACT

After defeating these Native American forces, the U.S. government tried to herd native populations onto **reservations** on the poorest land in the Dakotas, New Mexico, and Oklahoma to make room for the increasing number of white settlers. Pressured by reformers who wanted to "acclimatize" Native Americans to white culture, Congress passed the **Dawes Severalty Act** in 1887. The Dawes Act outlawed tribal ownership of land and forced 160-acre homesteads into the hands of individual Indians and their families with the promise of future citizenship. The goal was to assimilate Native

Americans into white culture as quickly as possible. As it turned out, the Dawes Act succeeded only in stripping tribes of their land and failed to incorporate Native Americans into U.S. society.

THE GRANGE

High protective tariffs and the Depression of 1893 had disastrous effects on poor **subsistence farmers** in the Midwest and South. Many of these cash crop farmers, often deeply in debt, were unable to afford the unregulated railroad fares to send their products to the cities. As a result, over a million impoverished farmers organized the **National Grange** to fight for their livelihood. The Grange managed to win some key victories in several midwestern legislatures, supporting the **Greenback Party** in the 1870s and then the **Populist Party** in the 1890s.

THE RISE AND FALL OF POPULISM: 1892–1896

EVENTS

1885	Farmers' Alliance forms
1891	Populist Party forms
1892	Grover Cleveland is elected president again
1893	Depression of 1893
1894	"Coxey's Army" marches on Washington, D.C. Congress passes the Wilson-Gorman Tariff Eugene V. Debs organizes Pullman Strike in Chicago
1895	J. P. Morgan bails out U.S. government
1896	William Jennings Bryan delivers "Cross of Gold" speech William McKinley is elected president
1897	Congress passes Dingley Tariff
1900	Congress passes Gold Standard Act

KEY PEOPLE

Grover Cleveland 22nd and 24th U.S. president; only president elected to two nonconsecutive terms

William McKinley 25th U.S. president; ran on pro–gold-standard platform against William Jennings Bryan in 1896

William Jennings Bryan Democratic congressman from Nebraska; won party's nomination for president in 1896 after giving famous "Cross of Gold" speech

Mark Hanna Wealthy Ohio businessman and McKinley's campaign manager in the elections of 1896 and 1900

James B. Weaver Former Civil War officer; Populist Party presidential candidate in 1892

J. P. Morgan Wealthy banker who saved U.S. government from bankruptcy in 1895 by loaning the Treasury more than $60 million

THE RISE OF THE POPULISTS

The **Populist movement** arose primarily in response to the 1890 **McKinley Tariff**, a very high tariff that particularly hurt western and southern farmers who sold their harvests on unprotected markets but were forced to buy expensive manufactured goods. To protest the tariff, these farmers helped vote Republicans out of the House of Representatives in the 1890 congressional elections.

By the time the elections of 1892 rolled around, the **Farmers' Alliance**—a quasi-political party that formed in the late 1880s—merged with other liberal Democrats to form the **Populist Party**. Populists nominated former Greenback Party member **James B. Weaver** for president and campaigned on a platform of unlimited, cheap silver money pegged at a rate of sixteen ounces of silver to one ounce of gold. Populists also campaigned for government ownership of all railroad and telephone companies, a graduated income tax, direct election of U.S. senators, one-term limits for presidents, immigration restrictions, shorter workdays, and a referendum.

THE ELECTION OF 1892

For the presidential election of 1892, the Republican and Democratic parties renominated candidates **Benjamin Harrison** and **Grover Cleveland**, respectively. In addition to the Populist candidate **James Weaver**, the fledgling **Prohibition Party** nominated **John Bidwell**. The Populists did surprisingly well, managing to receive over a million popular votes and twenty-two electoral votes. The unpopular McKinley Tariff ruined Harrison's chance for reelection, so Cleveland was reelected, improbably becoming the first and only president to serve two inconsecutive terms.

THE DEPRESSION OF 1893

Cleveland's second term was much more dynamic than his relatively uneventful first term, as the **Depression of 1893** hit just months after he took the oath of office. This depression, the worst the country had seen since the Depression of 1873, could not have come at a more desperate time for the federal government. On top of the fact that the U.S. Treasury was already nearly empty, wily investors traded silver for gold in a convoluted scheme that sent the **gold reserve** sinking below the $100 million mark. Had this trend continued, there would not have been enough gold to back the paper currency in circulation. The United States would have then had to go off the **gold standard**, which would have crashed the economy completely and ruined the country's financial credibility abroad.

J. P. MORGAN'S LOAN

To prevent any more gold from being used up, Cleveland repealed the 1890 **Sherman Silver Purchase Act,** much to the chagrin of Populist-leaning Democrats. But the act's repeal had little positive effect, and by the following year there was only $41 million left in the Treasury. The federal government thus was forced to look elsewhere for help. In a transaction that perhaps perfectly encapsulates the great power and wealth of big business in the Gilded Age, President Cleveland borrowed more than $60 million from Wall Street financier **J. P. Morgan** to put the U.S. economy back on solid ground.

COXEY'S ARMY

The Depression of 1893 and Cleveland's repeal of the Sherman Silver Purchase Act empowered the Populist movement, as disillusioned Democrats flocked to the Populist Party in the hopes of winning free silver and more power for the people. The depressed economic conditions also encouraged the creation of reform movements. In 1894, wealthy Ohio businessman **Jacob S. Coxey** set out with 500 men for Washington, D.C., to petition the federal government for cheap money and debt-relief programs. When **"Coxey's Army"** reached the Capitol building, however, the men were arrested for trespassing on the lawn.

BRYAN AND THE "CROSS OF GOLD" SPEECH

By 1896, Cleveland had virtually no chance of being elected for a third term. His presidency had been marred by a multitude of crises: he had failed to squelch the Depression of 1893, barely managed to keep the U.S. Treasury at a stable level, angered middle-class constituents by ending the Pullman Strike with federal forces, and not kept his promise to reduce the tariff significantly. As a result, Democrats instead nominated **William Jennings Bryan**, who at the nominating convention delivered his now-famous **"Cross of Gold" speech** in condemnation of the gold standard. In the speech, Bryan passionately proclaimed, "We will answer [the Republicans'] demands for a gold standard by saying to them: 'You shall not press down upon the brow of labor this crown of thorns; you shall not crucify mankind upon a cross of gold!'" Because the Democrats ran on a Populist-inspired platform, campaigning for free silver, the two parties joined in supporting Bryan.

MCKINLEY BUYS THE WHITE HOUSE

The Republican Party nominated Senator **William McKinley** of Ohio, sponsor of the controversial **McKinley Tariff**, on a pro-business platform. Wealthy Ohio businessman **Mark Hanna** financed most of the campaign and convinced his colleagues in the East to support McKinley. Hanna's expert politicking won McKinley the presidency despite Bryan's whirlwind speaking tour through the South and Midwest.

Ironically, Bryan's "Cross of Gold" speech, though seen as one of the finest rally cries in U.S. history, ended up creating many opponents of the free silver cause. Conservatives, fearing cheap money and inflation, flocked to the McKinley camp. The election of 1896 thus became less a race between Bryan and McKinley than a contest between those for Bryan and those against him. Wealthy business-men in the East invested about $15 million into McKinley's campaign, making it the largest campaign fund for a presidential candidate in history. Some Democrats quite reasonably claimed that McKinley had "bought" the White House.

THE FAILURE OF POPULISM

McKinley ultimately killed the Populists' dream of free silver in 1900 when he signed the **Gold Standard Act**, stabilizing the value of the dollar to one ounce of gold. In 1897, McKinley also signed the **Dingley Tariff** to set overall tariff rates at approximately 45 percent.

In retrospect, historians believe that the election of 1896 was one of the most important elections of the nineteenth century and certainly the most significant election since the Civil War. McKinley's win represented a victory for urban middle-class Americans over agrarian interests in the West and South. Populism never really spread into the cities, and Bryan's appeal for free silver and inflation alienated even the poorest Americans in the cities, who depended on a stable dollar to survive.

The Bryan campaign of 1896 essentially marked the end of the Populist movement, for the Populist Party effectively became a part of the Democratic Party by throwing its support behind Bryan. In addition, in light of Bryan's defeat, the election of 1896 marked the last time in which a major candidate tried to win by appealing to agricultural interests. McKinley's victory ushered in a new age in American politics in which conservatives dominated: Republicans would control the White House for the majority of the next thirty-six years.

SUMMARY & ANALYSIS

THE SPANISH-AMERICAN WAR: 1898–1901

EVENTS

1898	Anti-Imperialist League forms
	USS *Maine* explodes in Havana Harbor
	Spanish-American War begins
	United States annexes Hawaii
	Congress passes Teller Amendment
	Admiral Dewey seizes Philippines at Manila Bay
1899	Aguinaldo leads Filipino Insurrection
1900	Congress passes Foraker Act
	McKinley is reelected
1901	Insular Cases decided
	Congress passes Platt Amendment

KEY PEOPLE

William McKinley 25th U.S. president; asked Congress to declare war on Spain because he feared public opinion would turn against him

Theodore Roosevelt Assistant secretary of the Navy at outbreak of war; resigned and organized "Rough Riders" volunteer unit to fight the Spanish in Cuba

William Randolph Hearst Prominent "yellow journalist" who published sensational stories about atrocities in Cuba, inciting American public opinion against Spain

George Dewey Navy commander who launched a surprise naval attack on the Spanish fleet in Manila just hours after war began; defeated the Spanish in several hours without losing a single man

Emilio Aguinaldo Philippine freedom fighter; helped American forces defeat Spain in the Philippines but later turned against the United States

THE CRISIS IN CUBA

William McKinley entered the White House just as the nation was nearing a crisis with **Cuba**. Just ninety miles south of Florida, Cuba was still under Spanish control despite past American efforts to wrest it away. In the 1890s, falling sugar prices led Cuban farmers to rebel against their Spanish overlords in a bloody revolution. Spanish forces tried to crack down on the insurrection by herding all suspected revolutionaries, including children, into internment camps.

Americans became aware of the situation in Cuba via **"yellow journalists"** such as the famous newspapermen **William Randolph Hearst** and **Joseph Pulitzer**, who printed sensationalized stories about the events. In competition for readership, each man tried to outdo the other. Hearst, for example, sent painter **Frederick Remington** to Cuba with the order, "You furnish the pictures, and I'll furnish the war!" hoping to boost sales with exclusive coverage of the conflict.

THE USS MAINE

Already agitated by the articles of yellow journalists, Americans were outraged by the **Dupuy de Lôme letter**, which was intercepted and published in newspapers in 1898. In the letter, Spanish ambassador Enrique Dupuy de Lôme derided McKinley as a dimwitted politician. Inciting even greater public outrage, though, was the mysterious explosion of the **USS *Maine*** in Havana Harbor a week later, which killed more than 250 U.S. servicemen. American investigators concluded erroneously that a mine had destroyed the ship, despite Spain's insistence that there had been an accident in the ship's boiler room. Although history proved Spain correct, Americans rallied under the cry "Remember the *Maine*!" and clamored for war.

WAR PREPARATIONS AND THE TELLER AMENDMENT

Although McKinley did not want to go to war with Spain, he feared that if he failed to respond to strong public opinion for the war, William Jennings Bryan and his "free silver" platform would win the election of 1900. McKinley thus requested a declaration of war from Congress in April 1898; Congress consented on the grounds that the Cuban people needed to be liberated. To justify this cause, Congress passed the **Teller Amendment**, which promised Cuba independence once the Spaniards had been driven out.

THE PHILIPPINES

The resulting **Spanish-American War** was quick and decisive and crumbled the Spanish Empire. Acting against direct orders, Assistant Secretary of the Navy **Theodore Roosevelt**, an ardent expansionist, ordered Commodore **George Dewey** to seize the Spanish-controlled **Philippines** in Asia. Dewey defeated the Spanish fleet in a surprise attack on Manila Bay without losing a single man. Congress then annexed **Hawaii** on the pretext that the navy needed a refueling station between San Francisco and Asia. While Dewey fought the Spanish at sea, Filipino insurgent **Emilio Aguinaldo** led a revolt on land. Although Britain did not participate in the fighting, it did help prevent other European powers from defending Spain.

THE ROUGH RIDERS

The U.S. Army, meanwhile, prepared for an invasion of **Cuba** with over 20,000 regular and volunteer troops. The most famous of the volunteers were the **Rough Riders**, under the command of Lt. Colonel Theodore Roosevelt, who had left his civilian job to fight the "splendid little war." As the Rough Riders' name implied, they were an assortment of ex-convicts and cowboys mixed with some of Roosevelt's aristocratic acquaintances. Roosevelt and the Rough Riders helped lead the charge and take the famous **San Juan Hill** outside the city of Santiago. Cuba eventually fell, prompting Spain to retreat.

THE TREATY OF PARIS

In the **Treaty of Paris** that formally ended the war, Spain granted the United States Cuba, **Puerto Rico**, and **Guam**, and McKinley graciously agreed to buy the Philippines for $20 million. The United States did eventually honor the Teller Amendment and withdrew from Cuba in 1902, but not before including the **Platt Amendment** in the Cuban constitution, establishing a permanent U.S. military base at Guantánamo Bay.

POSTWAR HEADACHES

The war gave McKinley more headaches than it cured. First, McKinley was faced with an insurrection when Emilio Aguinaldo turned against American forces in the annexed Philippines. It took several years of jungle warfare before the insurrection was put down, but even then, Filipinos resisted assimilation into American culture.

Second was the problem of what to do with all the new people in the territories America had taken over. In 1901, the Supreme Court ruled in the **Insular Cases** that people in newly acquired foreign lands did not have the same constitutional rights as Americans living in the United States. Congress nonetheless upheld the 1900 **Foraker Act** that granted Puerto Ricans limited self-government and eventually full U.S. citizenship by 1917.

Finally, McKinley had to contend with the new, vocal **Anti-Imperialist League** and its prominent membership. The league challenged McKinley's expansionist policies and the incorporation of new "unassimilable" peoples into the United States.

ROOSEVELT'S BIG STICK DIPLOMACY: 1899–1908

EVENTS

1899	John Hay writes First Open Door Note
1900	U.S. sends troops to China to suppress Boxer Rebellion Hay drafts Second Open Door Note McKinley is reelected
1901	McKinley is assassinated; Theodore Roosevelt becomes president Hay-Pauncefote Treaty
1902	Colombia rejects canal treaty
1903	U.S. backs Panamanian revolt against Colombia Hay–Bunau-Varilla Treaty
1904	Roosevelt issues Roosevelt Corollary to the Monroe Doctrine Roosevelt is elected president Construction on Panama Canal begins
1905	United States invades Dominican Republic Roosevelt negotiates peace to end Russo-Japanese War
1906	San Francisco bans Japanese students from public schools Algeciras Conference United States invades Cuba
1907	Roosevelt sends Great White Fleet on world tour Roosevelt strikes "Gentlemen's Agreement" with Japan
1908	Root-Takahira Agreement
1914	Panama Canal is completed

KEY PEOPLE

William McKinley 25th U.S. president; reelected in 1900 but assassinated just months after inauguration in 1901

John Hay President McKinley's secretary of state; drafted Open Door Notes requesting that world powers respect free trade in Asia and China's territorial status

Theodore Roosevelt 26th U.S. president; took office after McKinley's assassination; adopted aggressive foreign policy and asserted American influence and power in the Western Hemisphere

SUMMARY & ANALYSIS

CHINA AND THE OPEN DOOR NOTES

In the aftermath of the Spanish-American War, the United States was presented with yet another problem—**China**. After losing the **Sino-Japanese War** of 1895, the Chinese could only sit back and watch as Japan, Russia, and the Europeans carved their ancient country into separate **spheres of influence**. U.S. policymakers, afraid that Americans would be left without any lucrative Chinese markets, scrambled to stop the feeding frenzy.

In 1899, McKinley's secretary of state, **John Hay**, boldly sent the **First Open Door Note** to Japan and the European powers, requesting that they respect Chinese territory and free trade. The British backed the agreement, but France, Germany, Russia, and Japan replied that they could not commit on the Open Door Note until all the other nations had agreed on it.

THE BOXER REBELLION

Chinese outrage over their country being divided up, regardless of whether it was conducted "fairly" or not, prompted a new nationalistic movement called the **Boxer Movement** to spread throughout China. In 1900, hoping to cast out all foreigners, the Boxer army invaded Beijing, believing that they would be divinely protected from bullets. They took a number of foreign diplomats hostage and waited patiently in the city. Nearly 20,000 French, British, German, Russian, Japanese, and American soldiers joined forces to rescue the diplomats and end the **Boxer Rebellion**. After the diplomats had been rescued, Secretary Hay issued the **Second Open Door Note** to request that the other powers respect China's territorial status, because he feared they would try to take revenge on the Chinese for the uprising.

THE ELECTION OF 1900 AND MCKINLEY'S ASSASSINATION

The election of 1900 turned out not to be much of a contest. Republicans renominated McKinley, who was popular because he had kept America prosperous and expanded the country as a result of the Spanish-American War. The Republicans also chose former Rough Rider Theodore Roosevelt to be McKinley's new running mate. Democrats again chose William Jennings Bryan on an anti-expansionism platform, but to their dismay, Bryan insisted once again on pushing for free silver—a stand that was partly responsible for his loss in the previous election.

Roosevelt and Bryan traveled throughout the country and played to the crowds in two whirlwind campaigns. In the end, free silver did in fact kill Bryan's chances again, and McKinley won the election with almost a million more popular votes and twice as many electoral votes.

However, only months into his second term, McKinley was **assassinated** by an anarchist while visiting the Pan-American Exposition in Buffalo, New York. He died a week later, and Vice President Roosevelt was sworn in as president.

Big Stick Diplomacy

Roosevelt, not one to shy away from responsibility or wait around for the action to start, immediately set to work. Unlike his predecessor, Roosevelt believed that the United States should always be prepared to fight. He applied his favorite proverb to the country: "Speak softly and carry a big stick, and you will go far," and bolstered the U.S. Army and Navy. Roosevelt's so-called **Big Stick Diplomacy** soon became synonymous with imperialism and aggressiveness, as his policy often took advantage of smaller and weaker nations.

The Panama Canal

One of Roosevelt's first goals was to construct a canal through the narrow Central American isthmus and link the Pacific and Atlantic oceans. In Colombia's northernmost province, **Panama**, Roosevelt struck a deal with rebels who were dissatisfied with Colombian rule, offering them independence and American protection in exchange for land to build the canal.

The rebels quickly consented and, in 1903, overtook the provincial capital while U.S. Navy ships prevented Colombian troops from marching into Panama. Roosevelt immediately recognized Panama's independence and sent Secretary of State John Hay to sign the **Hay–Bunau-Varilla Treaty**, which relinquished ownership of the canal lands to the United States. Construction on the **Panama Canal** began the following year and was completed in 1914.

The Roosevelt Corollary to the Monroe Doctrine

The Panama Canal was only the first step in Roosevelt's Big Stick diplomacy. Roosevelt further angered Latin Americans by adding his own interpretation to the **Monroe Doctrine** (the famous 1823 U.S. policy statement that warned European powers to stay out of Western Hemisphere affairs). Roosevelt's action was prompted when Venezuela and the Dominican Republic both defaulted on loans and several European nations sent warships to collect the debts by force.

Roosevelt, afraid that the European aggressors would use the outstanding debt as an excuse to reassert colonial influence in Latin America, did not want to take any chances. In 1904, he announced his own **Roosevelt Corollary to the Monroe Doctrine**, declaring that the United States would collect and distribute the debts owed to European powers—in effect stating that only the United States could intervene in Latin American affairs. Roosevelt then sent troops to the Dominican Republic to enforce debt repayment and to Cuba to suppress revolutionary forces in 1906.

RELATIONS WITH JAPAN

Relations between the United States and Japan soured during the Roosevelt years. In 1905, Roosevelt mediated a dispute between the Russians and the Japanese to end the **Russo-Japanese War**. Although these efforts won Roosevelt the Nobel Prize for Peace, both powers left the negotiating table unhappy and blamed Roosevelt for their losses. Ties to Japan were strained further when the **San Francisco Board of Education** banned Japanese students from enrolling in the city's public schools, giving in to popular anti-Japanese sentiments. Japanese diplomats in Washington, D.C., loudly protested the move, which led Roosevelt to make a **"Gentlemen's Agreement"** in 1907 stating that the San Francisco Board of Education would retract the ban as long as Japan reduced the number of immigrants to the United States.

In December 1907, in a show meant to demonstrate American prowess, Roosevelt sent sixteen U.S. battleships on a tour of the world. When the **Great White Fleet** stopped in Tokyo in 1908, Japanese and American officials signed the **Root-Takahira Agreement,** in which both countries agreed to respect the Open Door policy in China and each other's territorial integrity in the Pacific.

ROOSEVELT AND THE PROGRESSIVES: 1901–1908

EVENTS

1902	Anthracite Strike
	Congress passes Newlands Act
1903	Congress passes Elkins Act
1904	Lincoln Steffens publishes *The Shame of the Cities*
	Roosevelt creates U.S. Forest Service
	Northern Securities decision
	Industrial Workers of the World forms
	Roosevelt is elected president
1906	Upton Sinclair publishes *The Jungle*
	Congress passes Pure Food and Drug Act, Meat Inspection Act, and Hepburn Act
1907	"Roosevelt Panic" hits
1908	*Muller v. Oregon* case
	Taft is elected president

KEY PEOPLE

Theodore Roosevelt 26th U.S. president; launched a collection of progressive domestic policies known as the Square Deal

Robert La Follette Wisconsin governor and one of the most prominent progressives in the early 1900s

William Howard Taft 27th U.S. president; handpicked successor to Roosevelt in 1908

THE PROGRESSIVE MOVEMENT

By the dawn of the twentieth century, many Americans felt the need to change the relationship between government and society and address the growing social and political problems. Like the Populists before them, **Progressives** believed that unregulated capitalism and the urban boom required stronger government supervision and intervention. Specifically, Progressives wanted to regain control of the government from special interests like the railroads and trusts, while further protecting the rights of organized labor, women, blacks, and consumers in general.

Unlike the Populist movement, which rose from America's minority groups, Progressives came primarily from the middle class and constituted a majority of Americans in the Republican and Democratic parties. As a result, reform dominated the first decade of the new century.

THE MUCKRAKERS

At the forefront of the reform movement were turn-of-the-century exposé writers dubbed "muckrakers." These writers published the dirt on corporate and social injustices in books and magazines like *McClure's*, *Collier's*, and *Cosmopolitan*. Muckrakers had an unprecedented impact on public opinion and even on the president and Congress. For example, **Upton Sinclair**'s graphic description of the meatpacking industry in his 1906 novel ***The Jungle*** so deeply disgusted President Roosevelt and Congress that they passed the **Meat Inspection Act** and **Pure Food and Drug Act** the same year, hoping to clean up the industry and protect American consumers. In 1890, **Jacob Riis** awakened middle-class Americans to the plight of the urban poor in his book ***How the Other Half Lives***. Likewise, **Lincoln Steffens** published a series of articles titled **"The Shame of the Cities"** that further exposed big-business corruption.

PROGRESSIVES IN STATE GOVERNMENTS

In addition to operating in the federal government, Progressives also began to challenge industrial and political corruption at the state and local levels. Voters in many cities and states succeeded in their fight for **direct primary elections** and the **secret ballot** to eliminate bribes and reduce the power of political machines. Many states passed laws granting voters the power of **initiative**, or the right to directly propose legislation themselves; the **referendum**, allowing Americans to vote directly for or against specific laws; and the power to **recall** corrupt elected officials. Progressive governors like **Robert La Follette** of Wisconsin, **Hiram Johnson** of California, and **Charles Evans Hughes** of New York worked tirelessly to punish grafters, break up uncompetitive monopolies, and regulate public utilities.

THE SQUARE DEAL AND TRUST-BUSTING

An ardent Progressive himself, Roosevelt decided to use his powers to give Americans a **"Square Deal"** to protect the public interest. He focused his domestic efforts on regulating big business, helping organized labor, protecting consumers, and conserving the nation's already-dwindling natural resources.

Roosevelt began by launching a campaign to tackle monopolistic trusts that hurt consumers. In 1902, under the auspices of the Sherman Anti-Trust Act, he filed a lawsuit against James J. Hill's and J. P. Morgan's Northern Securities Railroad Company. In 1904, the Supreme Court upheld Roosevelt's suit in the **Northern Securities decision**, forcing the giant railroad company to disband. Roosevelt subsequently filed similar suits against dozens of other trusts, including the beef trust, the sugar trust, and the harvester trust.

Roosevelt also persuaded Congress to pass the **Elkins Act** in 1903, to punish railroad companies that issued uncompetitive rebates and the merchants who accepted them. To further the reform cause, in 1906, Congress passed the **Hepburn Act** to strengthen the Interstate Commerce Commission and give it more power to control the railroads.

LABOR PROTECTION

Roosevelt also earned the reputation of a friend to organized labor when he supported striking Pennsylvania coal miners in the 1902 **Anthracite Strike**. Fearing a coal shortage in the industrial eastern United States, the president offered to help mine owners and workers negotiate a settlement involving wages and work hours. When mine owners refused to negotiate, however, Roosevelt threatened to seize the mines and place them under the control of federal troops—the first time a U.S. president had ever sided with strikers against industrialists and forced them to compromise. The Supreme Court likewise sided with labor interests in its 1908 *Muller v. Oregon* ruling, which awarded some federal protection for female workers in factories.

CONSERVATION

During this era of reform, Roosevelt also pushed for **environmental conservation**. Fearing that Americans were on track to use up the country's natural resources, he set aside several hundred million acres of **forest reserves** and ore-rich land. He also convinced Congress to fund the construction of several dozen **dams** in the West and to pass the 1902 **Newlands Act**, which sold federal lands in the West to fund irrigation projects.

THE ELECTION OF 1908

Despite a brief financial panic in 1907, Roosevelt remained just as popular at the end of his second term as he was at the beginning of his first. However, after winning reelection in 1904, he had promised not to run again. Instead, he decided to endorse his vice president and close friend, **William Howard Taft**, a 350-pound giant of a man who Roosevelt believed would continue fighting for progressivism and the Square Deal. Meanwhile, Democrats nominated **William Jennings Bryan** yet again on an anti-imperialist, progressive platform. **Eugene V. Debs** also entered the race on the Socialist Party ticket. In the end, Taft easily defeated Bryan by more than a million popular votes and 150 electoral votes.

THE TAFT PRESIDENCY: 1909–1912

EVENTS

1909	Congress passes Payne-Aldrich Tariff
	New York City garment worker uprising
1910	Ballinger-Pinchot Affair
1911	Triangle Shirtwaist Company fire
	Standard Oil anti-trust case
	U.S. Steel Corporation anti-trust case
1912	Taft and Roosevelt split Republican Party
	Woodrow Wilson is elected president

KEY PEOPLE

William Howard Taft 27th U.S. president; alienated himself from fellow Republicans by
   supporting Payne-Aldrich Tariff and other non-progressive policies
Theodore Roosevelt Former U.S. president; split Republican Party in 1912 by running
   against Taft on Progressive Party ticket

TAFT'S DOLLAR DIPLOMACY

Whereas Theodore Roosevelt had employed "Big Stick" diplomacy
to bend weaker nations to his will, **William Howard Taft** preferred to
use money as leverage. Taft believed that he could convince smaller,
developing nations to support the United States by investing American dollars in their economies. **"Dollar Diplomacy,"** as pundits
dubbed it, not only made allies but also made money for American
investors.

Taft put his new policy to the test in **Manchuria**, where he
offered to purchase and develop the Manchurian Railway to prevent Russia and Japan from seizing control of it and colonizing
the region. However, both powers refused to hand the railway
over to the United States, and the deal quickly fell through. The
United States also dumped millions of dollars of investment into
unstable **Latin American countries** like Honduras, Nicaragua,
Cuba, and the Dominican Republic but eventually had to send
occupation troops to protect their investments. In short, Taft's
"Dollar Diplomacy" failed.

MORE TRUST-BUSTING

After these unsuccessful attempts at diplomacy, Taft devoted himself to domestic matters, making **trust-busting** his top priority.
Amazingly, he filed ninety lawsuits against monopolistic trusts in
just four years—more than twice as many as Roosevelt had filed in
a little less than eight years. In 1911, the Supreme Court finally used

the previously neglected **Sherman Anti-Trust Act** to dissolve John D. Rockefeller's **Standard Oil Company** for "unreasonably" stifling its competition. Later that year, Taft famously filed a lawsuit against J.P. Morgan's **U.S. Steel Corporation**. The lawsuit infuriated Taft's predecessor and political ally **Theodore Roosevelt**, who had helped form the company back in 1901.

THE PAYNE-ALDRICH TARIFF

Many Progressive Republicans hoped that Taft would keep his campaign promise to reduce the protective tariff. Although he tried, Taft did not have enough political clout to prevent conservatives within the party from repeatedly amending a bill for a lower tariff. By the time the **Payne-Aldrich Tariff** reached the president, conservatives had made so many amendments to keep tariffs high on certain products that the overall tariff rate had remained practically unchanged. In 1909, Taft signed the bill anyway and then hailed it as the best bill Republicans had ever passed. Outraged, Progressives denounced the tariff and called Taft a traitor.

THE BALLINGER-PINCHOT AFFAIR

Taft further alienated his supporters (and his friend Teddy Roosevelt) when he fired **Gifford Pinchot**, the head of the forestry division in the Department of Agriculture, for insubordination. Pinchot, a progressive, a personal friend of Roosevelt, and a popular conservationist, had angered Taft by opposing Secretary of the Interior **Richard Ballinger**'s decision to sell public wilderness lands in Alaska and the Rocky Mountains to corporate developers. Taft refused to reinstate Pinchot even after Roosevelt and several prominent Republicans appealed on his behalf. The 1910 **Ballinger-Pinchot Affair** thus blackened Taft's public image and earned him many enemies within his own party.

THE BULL MOOSE PARTY AND ELECTION OF 1912

Outraged by Taft's actions, Roosevelt, proclaiming that he was as "strong as a bull moose," founded the **Progressive Republican Party**, or **Bull Moose Party**, so that he himself could run against Taft on a third-party ticket in the presidential election of 1912. The Democrats, meanwhile, nominated Progressive **Woodrow Wilson**, who was a southerner by birth but had moved north to become the president of Princeton University and, later, governor of New Jersey. The proper and respectable Wilson championed a progressive package he called the **New Freedom** to tackle trusts and the high tariff.

Once again, former labor organizer **Eugene V. Debs** entered the race as the Socialist Party nominee.

In the end, the Roosevelt-Taft feud split the Republican Party and gave Wilson an easy win. Wilson received 435 electoral votes to Roosevelt's eighty-eight and Taft's eight. In a surprisingly strong showing, the Socialist candidate, Debs, managed to win nearly a million popular votes.

WILSONIAN PROGRESSIVISM: 1913–1916

EVENTS

1913	Sixteenth and Seventeenth Amendments are ratified Congress passes Federal Reserve Act and Underwood Tariff
1914	Panama Canal is completed Congress passes Clayton Anti-Trust Act, establishes Federal Trade Commission United States occupies Vera Cruz, Mexico
1915	Congress passes La Follette Seaman's Act United States invades Haiti
1916	Congress passes Workingmen's Compensation Act, Federal Farm Loan Act, Warehouse Act, Adamson Act, and Jones Act Pancho Villa attacks New Mexico United States invades Dominican Republic
1917	United States buys Virgin Islands

KEY PEOPLE

Woodrow Wilson 28th U.S. president; outlined New Freedom domestic policies to lower protective tariff and tame big business

Venustiano Carranza General who took power in Mexico after 1914 coup ousted revolutionary leader Victoriano Huerta

Pancho Villa Mexican rebel who tried to provoke war between the United States and Mexico in order to oust Venustiano Carranza from power

John J. Pershing General sent by Wilson to pursue Villa's band of Mexican rebels into Mexico in 1916

THE NEW FREEDOM

Even though **Woodrow Wilson** won the vast majority of electoral votes in the election of 1912, he received only 41 percent of the popular vote, ostensibly leaving him with little mandate. Despite this handicap, Wilson managed to accomplish every one of his major domestic goals on his progressive **New Freedom** agenda. In just four years, Wilson reduced the tariff, passed more anti-trust legislation, and reformed the banking system.

Wilson began in 1913 by pushing Congress to pass the **Underwood Tariff**, which drastically reduced duties on foreign goods from an average rate of 40 percent to an average rate of 25 percent. Congress compensated for the loss of revenue by creating a national income tax under the **Sixteenth Amendment**, another major progressive achievement of 1913.

BANKING REFORM

Next, Wilson took on the banking industry, which despite industrialization and the population boom had remained essentially unchanged since the Civil War. In 1913, Wilson and Congress passed the **Federal Reserve Act** to create a decentralized national bank comprising twelve regional branches. Collectively, all the private banks in each region owned and operated that respective region's branch. However, the new **Federal Reserve Board** had the final say in decisions affecting all branches, including setting interest rates and issuing currency. This new banking system helped stabilize national finances and credit and helped the financial system survive two world wars and the Great Depression.

OTHER PROGRESSIVE LEGISLATION

Wilson also continued to crack down on trusts, most notably by convincing Congress to pass the **Clayton Anti-Trust Act** in 1914. Unlike the Sherman Anti-Trust Act, the Clayton Anti-Trust Act actually gave lawmakers the power to punish monopolistic corporations. Furthermore, it legalized labor unions and their right to strike peacefully.

Congress passed a wide variety of other progressive legislation during Wilson's first term. The **La Follette Seaman's Act** of 1915, for example, protected sailors' rights and wages on merchant ships, while the **Federal Farm Loan Act** and the **Warehouse Act** of 1916 gave farmers access to easy credit. That same year, Congress also passed the **Workingmen's Compensation Act** to help support temporarily disabled federal employees and the **Adamson Act** to establish an eight-hour workday for all employees on interstate railroads. With the ratification of the **Seventeenth Amendment** in 1913, Americans won the right to elect U.S. senators directly.

WILSON'S FOREIGN POLICY

In foreign affairs, Wilson flatly rejected Roosevelt's Big Stick Diplomacy and Taft's Dollar Diplomacy in favor of a more moralistic approach to international relations. He immediately withdrew federal support for American investors abroad and pressured Congress to give increased (but not complete) control of the **Panama Canal** to Panama. In 1916, he signed the **Jones Act**, which made the Philippines an official U.S. territory and promised Filipinos independence once they established a stable government. Wilson did, however, send troops to Haiti, the Dominican Republic, and Cuba and purchased the U.S. Virgin Islands from Denmark in 1917.

CONFLICT WITH MEXICO

Wilson's greatest foreign policy challenge came from south of the border, after revolutionaries killed Mexico's president and replaced him with General **Victoriano Huerta** in 1913. Even though Wilson refused to bow to public pressure and declare war, he also refused to acknowledge Huerta's claim to power. However, when Mexican officials illegally arrested American sailors in 1914, Wilson ordered the navy to seize the port of **Vera Cruz**, Mexico.

Huerta's regime crumbled later that year, but another revolutionary, **Venustiano Carranza**, replaced him. In retaliation for the U.S. incursion at Vera Cruz, yet another rebel, **Pancho Villa**, took a small band of men and killed sixteen Americans while raiding a small town in New Mexico in 1916. Villa also hoped to start a war between his enemy Carranza and the United States. Under Wilson's orders, General **John J. Pershing** and several thousand army regulars invaded Mexico and crushed Villa's forces in 1916.

STUDY QUESTIONS & ESSAY TOPICS

Always use specific historical examples to support your arguments.

STUDY QUESTIONS

1. *How did railroads change American society, politics, and economy in the post–Civil War era?*

Railroads completely transformed the United States socially, politically, and economically during the Gilded Age. Literally the engine of the new industrialized economy, they facilitated the speedy transportation of raw materials and finished goods from coast to coast. In addition to raw materials, these "iron horses" carried people west to settle the heartland and the frontier. As the railroads grew in power, they exerted increasing influence on local and state governments, eventually prompting Congress and reform-minded presidents to pass laws to regulate the new industry.

After the Civil War, rail tycoons such as Cornelius Vanderbilt capitalized on the conversion of their iron tracks to steel, which allowed them to lay more track for only a fraction of the cost. As a result, by 1900, the United States boasted almost a quarter of a million miles of railroad track. In turn, steel magnates such as Andrew Carnegie benefited from the increased demand for steel and responded by producing more. As consolidation and innovation streamlined costs, it became cheaper and faster to ship raw materials, manufactured goods, foodstuffs, and oil via rail than by steamship.

Railroads transported people, too, and contributed, more than any other single factor, to the transformation and development of the West. Although more than a million Americans had moved westward in the days of "manifest destiny" before the Civil War, trains brought millions more throughout the latter half of the nineteenth century. Railways made it physically and economically feasible for Americans to settle Montana, Wyoming, Idaho, Arizona, New Mexico, Colorado, North and South Dakota, Nebraska, and Oklahoma in large numbers. At the same time, the decimated population of native grassland bison testified to the negative consequences of this drastic transformation of the Midwest.

As railroad companies grew in power, they exerted more and more influence on local politics and economics. Unscrupulous "robber barons" extorted the public by charging outrageous rates, distributing uncompetitive rebates to preferred customers, accepting bribes and kickbacks, and discriminating against small shippers. Public discontent with the railways emerged in small farming communities throughout the Midwest—a discontent that ultimately helped form the backbone of the populist movement. Populists, like the socialists of the early twentieth century, wanted to curb railroad corruption by nationalizing all lines.

Even though Populism eventually faded, cries for railroad reform did not, prompting the federal government to take action. In 1887, for example, Congress created the Interstate Commerce Commission (ICC), which supervised railroad companies that operated in more than one state by outlawing unfair rebates and ordering companies to publish fares up front. The Elkins Act of 1903 and the Hepburn Act of 1906 strengthened the ICC by restraining railroad companies further. In addition, the Supreme Court ordered the dissolution of James Hill's and J. P. Morgan's Northern Securities Railway in 1904.

Railroads thus transformed American society, politics, and economy unlike any other invention during the Gilded Age. They allowed big business to prosper and people to settle the West and Midwest. Ultimately, public reaction against the railroad barons' uncompetitive business practices formed the backbone of the reform-minded Populist and Progressive movements around the turn of the century.

2. *Many historians believe that the election of 1896 was the most critical election of the post–Civil War years. Do you agree with this assessment? How did the election change American politics?*

The election of 1896 was one of the most critical elections of the nineteenth century. William McKinley's victory over William Jennings Bryan brought an end to the Populist movement, ensured financial stability that helped industrialization, and ushered in a new era of Republican conservatism that lasted for nearly forty years. In addition, the election demonstrated the importance of money in national politics and the support of urban voters.

William Jennings Bryan's decision to incorporate much of the Populist Party platform into the Democratic Party platform effectively put an end to the Populist movement. Particularly important was Bryan's call for inflationary free silver to help impoverished farmers in the South and Midwest pay off their debts. Populist leaders chose to unite with Bryan and the Democrats rather than try to win with a third party candidate of their own. Although Bryan represented the best choice for winning that particular election, the Populist Party's support of him deprived them of their own platform and ultimately pushed many farmers permanently in line with the Democratic Party. The Populist Party never recovered and eventually dissolved completely.

However, both Populists and Democrats failed to realize that farmers no longer constituted the bulk of the American population. Even though the United States had been a predominantly agrarian country since the American Revolution, the industrialization and immigration of the Gilded Age shifted the population balance toward the cities. Bryan's appeal for inflationary silver worried urban residents, who relied on steady wages, and the free silver issue ultimately cost him the election. Consequently, the election of 1896 marked the last time a presidential candidate from a major party tried to win by appealing to agricultural interests. McKinley, on the other hand, appealed to American city dwellers, promising economic stability and a "full dinner pail" for every American. His sound money policies, which kept big business booming and the economy growing, ultimately helped the United States become the greatest industrialized nation in the world.

The election of 1896 also demonstrated the growing importance of money in American politics. With more than $15 million, McKinley had more money to spend on his campaign than any of his predecessors. He also had Mark Hanna, his wily campaign manager, who successfully convinced business tycoons to donate to the campaign. McKinley won the election in part because of his ability to spend more money, prompting many Democrats to accuse the former senator of "buying" his presidency.

Just as significantly, McKinley's victory ushered in a period in American politics dominated by Republican conservatism. In fact, Republicans controlled the White House for all but eight years between 1897 and 1933. Their fiscal conservatism and laissez-faire attitude toward the economy helped the American economy grow even further.

3.   *What were the causes of urbanization during the Gilded Age? What consequences did this urban revolution have on politics, the economy, and society?*

Rapid immigration, along with the explosion of Americans moving from farms to the cities, caused an urban boom during the Gilded Age. The growth of cities gave rise to powerful political machines, stimulated the economy, and gave birth to an American middle class.

Civil wars and persecution prompted many southern and eastern Europeans to flee their homelands in search of better lives in America between the 1880s and 1920s. During these years, approximately a million immigrants from Italy, Greece, Russia, Poland, and other countries arrived in eastern U.S. cities every year. In addition to the influx of immigrants, millions of country-dwelling Americans moved to the cities to escape poverty.

The urban explosion contributed significantly to the rise of powerful political machines that became synonymous with the Gilded Age. Political bosses like William "Boss" Tweed in New York City accumulated power and wealth by preying on insecure immigrants living in the cities' poorest slums. In exchange for their votes, bosses promised to provide social services, new public projects, and sometimes even physical protection. These political machines grew incredibly powerful well into the twentieth century and came to dominate local politics and even influence national politics. Nearly every U.S. president between Grant and Truman could trace their roots back to local and state party machines.

The shift in population from the countryside to the cities also changed the way presidential candidates campaigned, as demonstrated by William McKinley's victory over William Jennings Bryan in 1896. McKinley was able to secure the urban vote, which led him to victory, whereas Bryan wrongly assumed that the majority of the voting public was still in America's countryside.

The economy benefited greatly from the influx of immigrants and farmhands to the cities. Factory owners especially benefited from immigrants from southern and eastern Europe, who, eager to make a new start in America, often worked inhumane hours for meager wages and rarely threatened to unionize. The availability of such cheap labor contributed to the economic boom during the Gilded Age and throughout the early twentieth century.

The urban explosion, furthermore, contributed to the growth of a distinctive American middle class. Not rich but not poor either, a growing number of Americans could afford to live comfortably and enjoy the modern conveniences of Gilded Age life. The increasing number of middle-class women led to the reform movement of the late nineteenth century. Many of these women strove to eliminate poverty and right other social wrongs, such as drinking, prostitution, and gambling. Jane Addams, Lillian Wald, and other women founded settlement houses in urban slums to help immigrants improve their lives in the New World. This early reform movement served as the roots of the broader Progressive movement that dominated American politics after the turn of the century.

The veritable explosion in population between the 1880s and 1920s in eastern cities thus completely transformed American politics, society, and the economy. Politicians began campaigning harder in cities run by political machines, cheap labor fueled economic growth, and a distinctive American middle class emerged that would eventually spearhead the progressive movement.

SUGGESTED ESSAY TOPICS

1. *Why did the Populists gain so much power in the 1880s and 1890s, and why did they disappear soon after that?*

2. *Compare and contrast Roosevelt's Square Deal with Wilson's New Freedom.*

3. *What were the causes and consequences of Progressivism?*

4. *Describe how three of the following shaped American politics in the early twentieth century:*

    Ballinger-Pinchot Affair
    Payne-Aldrich Tariff
    muckrakers
    Underwood Tariff
    Square Deal
    Progressive Party

QUESTIONS & ESSAYS

Review & Resources

Quiz

1. Congress passed the Pendleton Act after

   A. The *Wabash* case
   B. The Battle of Wounded Knee
   C. The Battle of Little Big Horn
   D. The assassination of President Garfield

2. How did the Civil Service Commission eliminate the spoils system?

   A. By administering competitive exams to all applicants for federal jobs
   B. By hiring only applicants who were not in the same political party as the president
   C. By hiring only applicants whom the president did not personally know
   D. By reducing the number of available civil service jobs

3. Coxey's Army marched on Washington, D.C., in the hopes of winning

   A. Equal political rights for women
   B. Free coinage of silver
   C. Equal economic rights for blacks
   D. The right to unionize

4. Populists campaigned for all of the following *except*

   A. Free silver
   B. Nationalized railroads
   C. Social security
   D. A graduated income tax

5. The Pullman Strike of 1894

    A. Halted trains throughout the United States

    B. Made Eugene V. Debs a national figure

    C. Ended only after federal troops subdued the strikers

    D. All of the above

6. Some big businessmen such as Andrew Carnegie vertically integrated their corporations by

    A. Eliminating middlemen to control every aspect of production

    B. Buying out all competing firms to monopolize a single product

    C. Inflating the price of their own stock

    D. Issuing uncompetitive rebates

7. John D. Rockefeller of Standard Oil practiced horizontal integration by

    A. Eliminating middlemen to control every aspect of production

    B. Buying out all competing firms to monopolize a single product

    C. Inflating the price of his own stock

    D. Issuing uncompetitive rebates

8. What act of Congress was prompted by the Supreme Court's ruling in the 1886 *Wabash* case?

    A. Sherman Anti-Trust Act

    B. Interstate Commerce Act

    C. Pure Food and Drug Act

    D. Comstock Law

9. Why was the Sherman Anti-Trust act significant?

    A. The federal government used the act to break up several unfair monopolies

    B. It was the first piece of federal anti-trust legislation

    C. It represented the federal government's first attempt to regulate interstate commerce

    D. All of the above

10. The western frontier at the end of the nineteenth century was most transformed by

   A. The mechanical mower-reaper
   B. The Homestead Act
   C. The Dawes Severalty Act
   D. Railroads

11. The National Labor Union and the Knights of Labor were similar in that both represented

   A. Only skilled workers
   B. Only unskilled workers
   C. Both the skilled and unskilled
   D. Only urban laborers

12. Membership in the Knights of Labor dwindled after

   A. The Pullman Strike
   B. The Depression of 1873
   C. The Homestead Strike
   D. The Haymarket Square Bombing

13. The American Federation of Labor differed from the Knights of Labor in that

   A. The Knights accepted both skilled and unskilled laborers, whereas the AFL accepted only skilled
   B. The AFL accepted only skilled laborers, whereas the Knights accepted only unskilled
   C. The AFL accepted only farmers, whereas the Knights accepted laborers both in cities and on farms
   D. The AFL accepted skilled and unskilled laborers, whereas the Knights accepted only skilled laborers

14. From what region did most new immigrants in the United States come at the end of the nineteenth century?

   A. Germany and Ireland
   B. Latin America
   C. Asia
   D. Southern and eastern Europe

REVIEW & RESOURCES

15. Booker T. Washington and W. E. B. Du Bois disagreed on the issue of racial equality in that

   A. Washington fought for social and economic equality, whereas Du Bois fought primarily for social equality
   B. Du Bois fought for both social and economic equality, whereas Washington fought for only economic equality
   C. Washington strove for economic equality, whereas Du Bois fought only for social equality
   D. Du Bois fought for political equality in the South, whereas Washington fought for political equality in the North

16. Congress passed the Dawes Severalty Act in 1887 in order to

   A. Preserve Native American culture
   B. Put Native Americans on reservations
   C. Force Native Americans to assimilate into white American culture as quickly as possible
   D. Encourage all Native Americans to move to Canada

17. Upton Sinclair's novel *The Jungle* prompted Congress to pass the

   A. Warehouse and Adamson Acts
   B. Meat Inspection and Pure Food and Drug acts
   C. Foraker and Jones acts
   D. Newlands acts

18. What did historian Frederick Jackson Turner argue in 1893?

   A. The new wave of immigrants arriving in the United States was "unassimilable"
   B. Western expansion had had an enormous impact on American society and politics
   C. The Spanish-American war was an unjust war
   D. Women should not be allowed to vote because they were intellectually inferior to men

19. Why was President Garfield assassinated?

   A. A crazed Stalwart wanted Vice President Arthur to be president
   B. He had opposed civil service reform
   C. He had sent federal troops to end the Pullman Strike
   D. He had passed the McKinley Tariff

20. The Pendleton Act was passed to

   A. Lower the tariff rate from 50 percent to 30 percent
   B. Print more paper money to help poor farmers
   C. Control corrupt railroads
   D. Reform the spoils system

21. The McKinley Tariff raised the tariff rate to about

   A. 30 percent
   B. 40 percent
   C. 50 percent
   D. 60 percent

22. Why was the Republican Party politically weak throughout the Gilded Age?

   A. All the presidents were Democrats
   B. The bitter feuding between Half-Breeds and Stalwarts split the party
   C. Republicans could not agree how to reform the post–Civil War South
   D. Republicans were divided on the tariff issue

23. The Depression of 1893 depleted the U.S. Treasury so much that the federal government had to

   A. Give in to Populists' demands and coin silver
   B. Print more paper money
   C. Ask Wall Street for a loan
   D. Levy the first national income tax

REVIEW & RESOURCES

24. Tycoon Cornelius Vanderbilt transformed the railroad industry completely by

   A. Issuing unfair rebates
   B. Inventing the diesel locomotive
   C. Constructing the first transcontinental railroad
   D. Using steel tracks

25. In which case did the Supreme Court rule that only the federal government could regulate interstate trade?

   A. The *Northern Securities* case
   B. *Gideon v. Wainwright*
   C. The *Wabash* case
   D. *Roe v. Wade*

26. Which tycoon made steel into one of the nation's biggest industries?

   A. William Kelly
   B. Cornelius Vanderbilt
   C. Andrew Carnegie
   D. All of the above

27. Many middle-class Americans disliked labor unions in the late nineteenth century because

   A. They falsely associated organized labor with socialists
   B. They saw union members as ungrateful employees
   C. They saw strikers as violent anarchists
   D. All of the above

28. Why did membership in the National Labor Union fade in the mid-1870s?

   A. Most members joined the American Federation of Labor instead
   B. The Depression of 1873 made jobs scarce
   C. The economy boomed and workers didn't need to bargain for wages, hours, and better working conditions
   D. Americans didn't like labor unions in the 1870s

29. The Sherman Anti-Trust Act was most often used to prosecute

   A. Monopolistic corporations
   B. Labor unions
   C. Civil rights organizations
   D. Railroads

30. In which case did the Supreme Court legalize "separate but equal" public facilities for whites and blacks?

   A. The *Wabash* case
   B. *Brown v. Board of Education of Topeka, Kansas*
   C. *Plessy v. Ferguson*
   D. *Dred Scott v. Sanford*

31. Social Darwinists believed that

   A. Wealthy people were rich because they had gotten lucky
   B. Wealthy people were the best people
   C. The government should help eliminate poverty
   D. Everyone could become rich if they worked hard

32. Many farmers in the Midwest hated the railroad companies because they

   A. Issued unfair rebates to larger agricultural shippers
   B. Didn't publish standard fares
   C. Overcharged for even the shortest hauls
   D. All of the above

33. The Populist movement was born out of the

   A. Farmers' Alliance
   B. National Labor Union
   C. Communist Party
   D. Nativist League

34. Cleveland's second presidential term was plagued by all of the following crises *except*

    A. The Pullman Strike
    B. Coxey's Army
    C. Tweed Ring scandal
    D. Depression of 1893

35. Which of the following men delivered the famous "Cross of Gold" speech?

    A. William McKinley
    B. James Garfield
    C. Booker T. Washington
    D. William Jennings Bryan

36. The Populists' dream of free silver ended when Congress and McKinley passed

    A. The Gold Standard Act
    B. The Comstock Law
    C. The Pendleton Act
    D. The McKinley Tariff

37. What was the primary reason Benjamin Harrison lost the election of 1892?

    A. He was a Half-Breed
    B. He supported equal rights for blacks
    C. He had signed the McKinley Tariff
    D. He had passed the Comstock Law

38. Members of the Ghost Dance Movement sought to

    A. Turn away white settlers and return to traditional ways of life
    B. Resolve differences with whites and assimilate into white American culture as quickly as possible
    C. Increase cultural awareness of Native American traditions among whites
    D. Move all Native Americans to Canada

39. Roosevelt's Corollary to the Monroe Doctrine effectively stipulated that

   A. European powers could establish no new colonies in the Western Hemisphere
   B. The United States could seize any land it needed in order to complete the Panama Canal
   C. The United States would relinquish all claims to Cuba after winning the Spanish-American War
   D. Only the United States could intervene in Latin American affairs

40. All of the following inventions transformed American life in the late 1800s *except*

   A. The lightbulb
   B. The automobile
   C. The skyscraper
   D. The telephone

41. What was the main reason Woodrow Wilson won the election of 1912?

   A. Americans supported his Progressive policies
   B. Taft and Roosevelt divided Republican voters
   C. Americans feared socialists, revolutionaries in Mexico, and a growing Germany
   D. Taft had alienated too many voters

42. With which Native American tribes did the United States fight wars?

   A. Nez Percé
   B. Sioux
   C. Apache
   D. All of the above

43. Which of the following affected African Americans most directly?

   A. The Pendleton Act
   B. The Comstock Law
   C. The McKinley Tariff
   D. The *Plessy v. Ferguson* decision

44. Farmers were represented by all of the following *except*

   A. The Farmers' Alliance
   B. The Grange
   C. The McKinley Tariff
   D. The Populist movement

45. Roosevelt announced his Corollary to the Monroe Doctrine out of fear that

   A. European countries would use unpaid debts to exert influence in Latin America
   B. Pancho Villa would launch another raid on U.S. territory
   C. Spain would kill more Cuban civilians
   D. Victoriano Huerta would seize power in Mexico

46. Whom did Jane Addams's Hull House strive to help?

   A. Urban immigrants
   B. Urban blacks
   C. Suffragettes
   D. Native Americans

47. As the head of which institution did Booker T. Washington push for improved education for blacks?

   A. Howard University
   B. Emory University
   C. The Tuskegee Institute
   D. American University

48. John Hay's Open Door Notes requested that Japan and Europe

    A. Stay out of Latin American affairs
    B. Respect China's territorial status and the principle of free trade
    C. Reduce their number of warships according to a 5:3:1 ratio
    D. Maintain the territorial status quo in Southeast Asia

49. Taft alienated progressive Republicans and voters by supporting the

    A. Payne-Aldrich Tariff
    B. Underwood Tariff
    C. McKinley Tariff
    D. Dingley Tariff

50. Theodore Roosevelt's Square Deal domestic agenda called for

    A. Protecting consumers from harmful trusts
    B. Helping organized labor
    C. Conserving natural resources
    D. All of the above

SUGGESTIONS FOR FURTHER READING

CASHMAN, SEAN DENNIS. *America in the Gilded Age: From the Death of Lincoln to the Rise of Theodore Roosevelt*. New York: New York University Press, 1993.

HINE, ROBERT V., AND JOHN MACK FARAGHER. *The American West: A New Interpretive History*. New Haven, Connecticut: Yale University Press, 2000.

LAFEBER, WALTER. *The New Empire: An Interpretation of American Expansion, 1860–1898*. Ithaca, New York: Cornell University Press, 1998.

LINK, ARTHUR S., AND RICHARD L. MCCORMICK. *Progressivism*. Wheeling, Illinois: Harlan Davidson, 1983.

MCMATH, ROBERT C. *American Populism: A Social History, 1877–1898*. New York: Hill and Wang, 1990.

SCHLERETH, THOMAS J. *Victorian America: Transformations in Everyday Life, 1876–1915*. New York: Perennial, 1992.